RUNNING
AND
RACING
AFTER 35

Books by Allan Lawrence and Mark Scheid

THE SELF-COACHED RUNNER
THE SELF-COACHED RUNNER II
RUNNING AND RACING AFTER 35

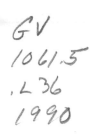
RUNNING
AND
RACING
AFTER 35

Allan Lawrence
and Mark Scheid

LITTLE, BROWN AND COMPANY
BOSTON   TORONTO   LONDON

Before embarking on any strenuous exercise program, including the
training described in this book, everyone, particularly those with known
heart or blood-pressure problems, should seek medical clearance from
a physician, preferably one with sports medicine experience.

Line drawings by Connie Coffelt-Lawrence

Library of Congress Cataloging-in-Publication Data

Lawrence, Allan.
    Running and racing after 35 / Allan Lawrence and Mark Scheid. —
1st ed.
        p.   cm.
    1. Running — Training. 2. Running races. 3. Running —
Psychological aspects. 4. Middle age. I. Scheid, Mark.
II. Title. III. Title: Running and racing after thirty-five.
GV 1061.5.L36   1990
796.42 — dc20   89-29992
                                                       CIP

10 9 8 7 6 5 4 3 2 1

RRD-VA

Published simultaneously in Canada
by Little, Brown & Company (Canada) Limited

Printed in the United States of America

For my daughters, Kristine Dianne and Sharon Kay, and my wife, Connie, who runs beside me on the gun lap.

—A.L.

Once again, for Mary, Troy, and Claire.

—M.S.

Contents

Acknowledgments

A number of people have contributed to the successful production of *Running and Racing After 35*. Especially noteworthy are the contributions of Frances Baxter, Connie Coffelt-Lawrence, Kirk Coverstone, Dr. Herbert L. Fred, Bruce Glikin, George Lyon, and the participants in the surveys that led to the completion of the stress evaluation form. Mary Scheid provided, as always, useful advice and insight. Additionally, our thanks go to the staff of the Institute for Aerobics Research, Dallas, Texas, for the circuit training program in chapter 2. We are grateful for the incisive comments of longtime track writer and expert commentator Jim Dunaway. At Little, Brown, we have enjoyed the cheerful assistance of Dana Groseclose and Peggy Freudenthal in the preparation of the manuscript; and, as always, we are grateful to Ray Roberts for having had the foresight to acquire us as Little, Brown authors.

We would especially like to acknowledge the contributions of all the over-35 runners and racers who have achieved — or who will achieve — their goals through the information and training system contained herein. Thank you, and best of luck.

Introduction

"He who competes against time has an adversary who does not suffer casualty." When Samuel Johnson wrote these words, he was no doubt thinking about the missed deadline for his dictionary, but the statement sums up neatly the central problem athletes face.

Athletes compete against time in two ways. The most obvious is when an athlete tries to achieve his or her best performance — in the struggle for a personal best, a school record, or a world record, depending on the athlete's ability. The more insidious effect of time on athletic performance is, in the traditional view, an athlete's inability to continue to compete after the "peak years" are passed.

But the definition of the "peak years" has undergone a gradual aging itself in the eighty years or so that the question has been considered. The first champions in the modern Olympics were mostly American university undergraduates; it was widely believed that age 21 was the last good year for amateur athletes and the time to "put away childish things" such as sport. This attitude persisted in the United States, where college graduation routinely marked the end of an athlete's competition. In the middle decades of this century, however, other nations came to regard this as typical of America's "throwaway" mentality. As a result, their athletes trained and competed into their twenties, and in international competition it gradually became clear that college undergraduates are physiologically inferior to athletes in their late twenties. Currently the ages of 27 through 30 are tacitly accepted as the "peak years."

This widely accepted "wisdom" too has been challenged, by a number of athletic performances in the last several years. In the 1984 Los Angeles Olympics, most of the pre-race speculation in the men's marathon centered on the expected duel between 27-year-old World Champion Rob de

Castella of Australia and the 26-year-old world-record-holder Alberto Salazar of the United States. But the gold medalist was Carlos Lopes, a 36-year-old Portuguese runner. His victory, an Olympic Record of 2:09:21, surprised the physiological pundits who flatly stated before the race that Lopes was "too old" to compete against the younger world-class runners. Lopes's race ushered in an era of remarkable performances by masters* runners. Taken together, these performances indicate a need to revise current thinking about age limitations on physical ability.

Two events of November 1987 are good examples: The women's race in the New York Marathon was won by 43-year-old Priscilla Welch of Great Britain (whose best time of 2:26:51 would have won a medal in thirteen of the twenty *men's* Olympic marathons to date). In the World Seniors Games in Melbourne, Derrick Turnbull, a 60-year-old New Zealand dairy farmer, won his races in the 800 meters (2:17), the 1,500 meters (4:27), the 5,000 meters (16:58), the 10,000 meters (35:11), the 10,000 meter cross-country race, and the marathon (2:41), and capped his outstanding achievement with a win in the handicap mile over all the winners in other age groups.

As Turnbull's races indicate, breakthroughs in over-40 human performance are not limited to the distance events. In August 1988, in the U.S. Masters Track and Field Championships in Orlando, Florida, five runners broke the then-existing masters outdoor record of 4:16, with John Bell of England winning in 4:12 in hot and humid conditions. In May of 1989, miling great Wilson Waigwa ran 4:07 for a mile, a few months after turning 40. Almost certainly the next few years will see the first masters sub-four-minute mile. The question is who will be first to break the barrier — one of the great milers of the past (Jim Ryun, Len Hilton) who are training for the event, or one of the current miling superstars who are reaching what was once thought to be "advanced age" for a miler (John Walker, for instance, ran 3:54 at age 38).

We are thus in the midst of a revolution in our thinking about the effect of aging on athletic performance. And, since aging was always believed to

---

* Exactly what to call older runners has posed a problem to national and world governing bodies. The Athletics Congress (TAC/USA), the governing body for U.S. running and race-walking, defines over-40 men and women as "masters"; men and women aged 30 to 39 compete as "sub-masters." The World Association of Veteran Athletes (WAVA), the major international governing body, calls male runners over 40, and females over 35, "veterans." Male participants in the Senior Olympics must be over 55, although TAC calls runners over 18 "seniors," to distinguish them from under-18 "juniors." In this book, for convenience, we use "masters" to mean runners who are susceptible to the problems caused by the aging process: most runners over 35.

diminish athletic performance first and most severely, we also by extension need to revise our thinking about aging in general.

This book is designed to be the first comprehensive review of the effect of the aging process on sports, on running in particular, and the strategies competitive runners can adopt to avoid the negative effects of aging on their competitive running.

The first chapter reviews the current scientific knowledge on the effects of aging on athletes, and more specifically, on runners. It is becoming obvious that the previously predicted physiological limits are inaccurate. Where are the real limits? To what extent are the effective limitations psychological and sociological rather than physiological? Given these aging-related problems, what should a masters runner do? The second half of our first chapter discusses the philosophy and practice of training and racing for masters.

Chapter 2 begins a systematic discussion of the recommendations made in the first chapter. Stretching, strength work, and massage serve as the first line of defense for masters runners; this chapter gives specific illustrated examples of what to do and how.

Chapter 3 focuses on a topic that has had a lot of coverage in the popular press for the last ten years: diet and nutrition. Which of the thousands of diets is the best for runners? Is it really possible to "eat to win"?

The fourth chapter addresses arguably the most important subject of all for masters runners: sports psychology and competition. One of the lessons we can learn from the recent performances of masters runners is that we are limited by our cultural and sociological expectation that we'll inevitably slow down as we get older. But when the first masters four-minute mile is run, what excuse will we have? This chapter also contains a questionnaire that can help runners evaluate their own stress levels (both athletic and nonathletic) to help them monitor their own training stresses.

In chapters 5, 6, and 7, the schedules are given for the three most popular race distances in America: 5,000 meters, 10,000 meters, and the marathon. The schedules are designed with two purposes in mind. First, the times provided supplement rather than replace the schedules in our earlier books. (For example, *The Self-Coached Runner II* provides schedules for running a five kilometer race in 15, 16, 17 minutes and so on. In response to our readers' requests, this book provides schedules for the intervening half-minute times — 15:30, 16:30, etc.) More important, the schedules are written with new knowledge and awareness of the effects of the aging process on runners and are designed to be used in conjunction with the Stress and Competition questionnaire in chapter 4.

The last chapter, "Questions and Answers," provides a compilation of information interesting to masters runners, especially answers to often-asked questions, such as "Could a masters runner participate in an Olympic event?" (It's already happened several times.), and predictions: When will the first masters sub-four-minute mile be run?

This book, like its predecessors, teaches you to train yourself, without becoming bogged down in a mass of scientific information — and also, like its predecessors, stresses improvement that will not depend upon chance, but upon you, the self-coached masters runner. We hope that you find *Running and Racing After 35* helpful and informative, and that it provides you with the information and motivation you need to make your own running as good as it can be.

PART I

PREPARATION

CHAPTER 1

The Aging Process and What to Do About It

THE AGING PROCESS has been under scientific investigation for almost a hundred years, but to date there is little agreement even on the mechanism by which it takes place. There are, however, a number of leading theories, which we'll briefly discuss here, along with their implications for the competitive runner.

As we were reviewing the literature on various theories of aging, we were struck by the fact that the threats to the microcosm of the cell had easily recognized parallels in the threats to the macrocosm of the earth as a political or ecological entity. For your interest, and because it may make the theories easier to understand and to keep separate, we introduce each aging theory with the heading of the appropriate parallel "world problem."

Terrorism: The *free-radical* theory is so called because the metabolism of cells produces, as part of its normal processes, certain "free radicals" — fragments of broken-down molecules — inside the cell. These bounce around randomly, causing damage to the molecules they touch, often producing more free radicals as a result of this molecular damage, in a domino effect. Organisms that naturally have a relatively high metabolic rate (such as mice) have a much higher level of free-radical production than humans; organisms with a slower metabolic rate have lower levels than humans. Proponents of the free-radical theory have argued that this difference in the level of free-radical production accounts for the fact that small animals (which tend to have high metabolic rates) have shorter lives than animals with lower metabolic rates, like giant tortoises. Additionally, giving animals antioxidants (like vitamins C and E) can slow their aging process, but there is no proof as yet that these vitamins have the same effect in humans. Some researchers also suggest that free-radical damage is the source of many degenerative diseases, such as cataracts, atherosclerosis, and even cancer.

The genetic time bomb: Other theorists, while agreeing that "live fast, die young" is a natural fact, attribute this timetable to a *cellular (or genetic) clock.* The cellular-clock theory was developed by a biologist named Leonard Hayflick, who found that — in contrast to then-current biological theory — a colony of cells *couldn't* be kept alive indefinitely when they were provided with optimum conditions. In fact, Hayflick found that animal cells would continue to divide, grow, and redivide only a limited number of times before the process ceased and the cell line died out. Furthermore, the number of times a cell could divide (called the Hayflick limit) varies according to the usual life span of various species. (For humans, the Hayflick limit is around 50 divisions; for Galápagos tortoises, the Hayflick limit is between 90 and 125.) This implies that *something* is happening inside the cell; otherwise, how does it know when its time's up? By implanting the nuclei of older cells into younger cells, which then showed the "life expectancy" of cells of the same age as the nucleic material, Hayflick was also able to demonstrate that the cell nucleus is the location of the "clock." (Here proponents of the free-radical theory suggest that no clock mechanism is needed; the breakdown in cell life, they say, can be explained by free-radical-produced genetic damage.)

There are, according to proponents of other theories of aging, several problems with the theory of genetic control of the aging mechanism. First, while it is widely accepted that genes can shorten life — that humans can inherit a genetic tendency toward diabetes and other life-shortening diseases — it has never been demonstrated that there exist such things as "good genes," that can contribute to longevity. Specialists in evolutionary theory contribute another argument: natural selection does not seem to operate in favor of producing organisms that far outlive their date of sexual maturity. Once an animal's genes are passed on to the next generation, nature "doesn't care" what happens to that particular animal, so there is no natural-selection pressure in favor of old organisms (no matter how attached we, as individuals, are to our own lives).

Spaceship earth: Another school of thought, accordingly, is that cells die because they can't keep up with the molecular garbage they produce — not the free radicals, just their used-up proteins. As cells age, they become less efficient in taking the garbage out. As the garbage piles up, the cell becomes less and less efficient and finally dies of the accumulation of metabolic waste.

Subversion from within: As the body ages, the immune system decreases in effectiveness, probably because the thymus gland decreases from a large size in adolescence to just barely visible at age 50. In fact, some researchers suggest that the immune system begins to produce increased antibodies to the body's *own* tissue. Studies show that a reduced diet may help to overcome this tendency.

Effects of the Aging Process

Whatever the causes of the aging process, there is little debate over its effects. As you read about them, however, you should remember that, to date, almost all research on aging has involved studying "normal, average" people — that is to say, people who get less and less exercise as they get older. Some of these effects may apply to runners, some may not — we don't know for sure.

Flexibility decreases as your tissues become less elastic and stiffer. In some cases, your joints may suffer impaired range of motion, too, which contributes to loss of flexibility.

Your *strength* declines. You're born with a certain number of muscle cells. As you age they die off and are not replaced. At the same time — studies of "average" people show — muscles suffer an increase in fat, water, and nonmuscle tissue.

You lose *cardiovascular efficiency*. At age 50, the normal sedentary person will have only 80 percent of the cardiovascular efficiency he had when he was 30. By age 70, the average person is down to 70 percent. In nearly all Americans, this problem is compounded by arteriosclerosis, or narrowing and hardening of the blood vessels, a condition we believe is caused in large part by diet.

Paralleling these declines is a drop in *lung capacity*. If you are an average person, your lung capacity at age 50 would be only 75 to 80 percent of its level when you were 30. The decrease in your pulmonary capacity is further aggravated by the fact that your chest has become stiffer over time, so it can't expand as fully as before. And the muscles that expand your chest and lower your diaphragm to make you inhale are weaker than they were when you were younger.

The speed of your *nerve impulses* decreases over time, but at a relatively slow rate: 10 percent over your life, about 5 percent between ages 30 and 50. Even that little is enough for athletes to "lose a step," as the saying goes.

Put this way, it seems a bleak picture: you may think you're going to become a mere shadow of your former self as you age. If you believe that to be true, of course, it will happen — because not even the combined physical effects of the aging process are as devastating to the athlete as are the *psychological effects*. If you believe that you will slow down, you *will* slow down — that is a running truism no matter what your age!

Fortunately, there are good reasons to believe that you *can* run as well (or in some cases better) as you age, *if* you take the physical and psychological factors into consideration and adjust your training to overcome the slowing-down process of aging.

Training to Fight Aging

Besides the specific programs given in the following chapters, there are several important questions that we find every runner over 35 confronts (consciously or unconsciously). These questions concern the following issues of training philosophy.

WHAT TRAINING METHOD SHOULD I USE?

Nearly every competitive runner wonders, as she gets older, whether or not the program that has enabled her to run well in the past will still work for her. Is it enough merely to modify, or should she embark on a different training program, one somehow "designed" for older runners?

The answer, expressed in its simplest form, is "Dance with who brung you." If you have had successful training in the past, you can expect the same form of training to benefit you now and in the future. The training philosophy and the schedules included in this book have been tested over many years and have been successful in producing the desired result: improved performance among a wide range of athletes of both sexes, of differing abilities, and of all ages.

For those runners over 35 who are just beginning competitive training, here is a summary of the factors that determine inherent racing ability:

Speed is the ability to run quickly over short distances, usually 220 yards or less. (Because of the loss of muscle strength and flexibility usual with age, speed is one factor in racing that requires the greatest training modification. On the other hand, it is the least important of the four components for the racing distances discussed in this book.)

Anaerobic capacity is the ability to withstand oxygen debt. It is primarily a function of the levels of certain enzymes in the blood. Since those enzyme levels vary according to the presence or absence of specific training, this component should vary little with age. However, aging can cause a small decrease in a runner's endurance (see below), and this change can affect anaerobic capacity indirectly.

Endurance, as we define it, is the ability to run distances — usually greater than a mile — at a maximal heart rate without incurring a debilitating oxygen debt. This component of racing capability is usually less affected by aging than speed is.

Stamina we define as the ability to run long distances without seriously taxing the cardiovascular or muscular systems. Stamina is the least age-affected of all the inherent capacities.

IF I LOSE MORE SPEED THAN ANYTHING ELSE, SHOULDN'T I DO MORE SPEED TRAINING TO MAKE UP FOR IT?

Although this seems like a logical approach, such a step will probably hurt your racing. Observation has shown that the less inherent speed that runners have, the less speed training they can tolerate — and this is true whether the runners are slowed because of a low percentage of fast-twitch fiber or because of the effects of age. (Muscles are composed of slow-twitch [ST] and fast-twitch [FT] fibers. Distance runners need a high percentage of ST fibers, which contract slowly and weakly but recover quickly; sprinters, a high percentage of FT fibers, which contract strongly and quickly but tire rapidly.) Additionally, speed training carries an increased risk of injury for the older athlete.

All this does *not* mean that you should eliminate speed training. On the contrary, you need it (even at the distances of five kilometers and beyond addressed in this book) to have the ability to surge in the middle of a race, to outsprint a competitor to the finish, and most of all, to maintain a training program that balances all four of the racing components described above.

Mac Stewart, track runner for 35 years. (Photograph by Conrad J. Mc-Carthy)

SHOULD I AT LEAST STAY OFF THE TRACK, THEN?

Track work becomes more important than ever, once the runner passes age 35. Besides the benefits of proper speed training and consequent increases in strength, the track also provides a superb venue for giving discipline and structure to a training regimen. At the same time, the accurate distances on the track allow a runner to monitor exactly her performance in training and offer good insurance against an old enemy that becomes more deadly with age: overtraining (see below).

Many of our readers who live in the Northeast and the Midwest have asked us about training in areas of the country where tracks are unusable during much of the winter. Even if tracks are kept free of snow, the bitter winter cold may require runners to wear clothing that limits the free movement needed in speed work.

If you are affected by these conditions, you should make the following adjustments:

- Find a trail or road that is usually cleared of snow (and free from ice).
- Measure a number of distances from 110 yards to 1 mile, using easily identifiable landmarks (trees, poles, hydrants, shrubs, gates, etc.) as starting and finishing points. These distances do not have to be exact but should be reasonably accurate (at a 6-minute pace, every 10 yards mismeasured changes your mile split 2 seconds).
- If you do not have measured distances, run the effort called for in your schedule on a time basis — that is, if your schedule calls for 440s in 90 seconds with a 440 recovery, run 90 seconds of effort, then jog for 2 minutes 30 seconds before your next effort.
- If you are heavily dressed because of the cold, run your efforts with the wind at your back to compensate for the extra clothing.

While there are obvious limitations to not having a track available year-round, there is no reason that a runner who is restricted by severe winter conditions cannot salvage the necessary speed workouts using these methods.

ARE THERE ANY PARTICULAR HAZARDS FOR THE OVER-35 RUNNER?

The most important hazard is a nebulous and negative one: *overtraining* has more serious consequences for the over-35 runner, and it is harder to avoid because the margin for error is smaller.

All runners probably know some other runner who has always had the uncanny ability to "bash himself into shape" in five or six weeks. No matter how out of shape this character got, you knew that he would show up for the big race trim and fit, and bury you. When you asked him what he did to turn his racing around in that length of time, he'd just say, "Well, everyone knows you have to train hard to race hard, so I just did two track workouts a day, took a long hard run on the weekend, and tried to total 80 miles a week."

With very few exceptions, this ability to "bash" is limited to younger runners. So as you and your nemesis enter new age groups, he's going to have to adopt a more sensible training program (such as yours) or get used to watching the race from the sidelines with an injury. And his new situation is a helpful reminder for all of us: the body's ability to tolerate overtraining stress seems to be reduced with age and, combined with the other aging factors, predisposes the unwary or the overconfident to injury. Be careful not to run your track times too much faster than suggested, don't try to double up on the mileage because "more is better," and above all, use the recovery days in your schedule to *recover*.

The price of combining serious training with increased age is eternal vigilance. As one masters runner puts it, "An old car may be just as fast now as it was when it was new, but you need to check under the hood more often."

I CAN UNDERSTAND AND TRAIN TO OVERCOME THE PHYSICAL CHANGES SINCE I TURNED 35, BUT MY PROBLEM IS THAT I JUST DON'T SEEM TO GET AS "PSYCHED-UP" FOR RACES AS I USED TO.

It would seem logical that the "slowing-down" consequences of the aging process would be the toughest obstacle to overcome when a runner enters the masters ranks, but — generally speaking — this is not the case. A far greater problem is that of individual "conscience."

Here's how this personally imposed barrier usually works:

You've reached your mid-thirties and you realize that your ability to compete in "open" competition has diminished. Your chances of placing in the top ten in local races, making the Olympic qualifying standard, or competing in the Olympics themselves are dreams and goals of the past. From an economic point of view your livelihood does not depend on your ability to win races, and perhaps you have pressure from various sources urging you that now is the time to "stop the running nonsense and get on with the rest of your life." For the past several years, however, running has been an important and normal part of your lifestyle, and you have grown to love the feelings that racing and training provide. Now, at this critical period, can you justify your need and desire to continue your sporting life? Isn't it time for you to concentrate on your career, your family, a personal relationship?

The way you feel about these or similar questions will have a definite bearing on the effectiveness of your entry into the masters ranks. Unfortunately, many runners feel that they might be acting selfishly if they continue with the same commitment to their racing and training. These feelings often result in an ambivalent attitude toward competition, which in turn causes a greater loss in racing performance than aging itself does. This "poor performance," in the eyes of the runner, reinforces the thought that he's "past his prime" and ought to "put away childish things," and the cycle begins again.

When runners I coach express these feelings to me, I have no hesitation in assuring them that continuing with their running and competitive activities is not, and should not be, a threat to relationships, family, or job. I try to point out the many beneficial aspects of continuing with their sport: Job situations can benefit from the discipline, structure, controlled aggressiveness, and energy generated by competition. Family and emotional relationships can be strengthened through better time management and a greater appreciation of the importance of mutual cooperation and support.

To be successful, then, the number-one requisite for the over-35 athlete should be a "guilt-free" attitude toward racing and training with the incorporation of sound philosophical and practical training methods as the runner prepares to enter the masters ranks.

Beating the Aging Process: A Specific Program

Within the context of our training philosophy, and incorporated in the schedules in this book, the way to counteract the aging process lies in attacking each of the specific problems that may come with age.

To overcome your loss of strength and flexibility, you will need to turn to strength training and stretching (even if you never had to do so before). To further counter your loss of flexibility, and to help avoid injury, you'll need to add massage to your training regimen.

To guard against the weight gain common in older people, you'll have to watch your diet, and you'll need to do so in a way that also cuts down on cholesterol and saturated fats, which decrease your cardiovascular efficiency (besides being linked to an increased risk of heart disease). Yet, at the same time, your diet needs to provide you with enough energy, vitamins, and minerals so that you'll be strong enough to run well.

Finally, in order to run your best, you'll need to develop a systematic pattern of psychological strengthening and stress evaluation, so that you can counter many of the negatives involved in being a competitive runner past the age of 35.

We discuss these countermeasures in the following chapters on the philosophy and practice of training. The next chapter deals with the first step you need to take: countering the direct physiological effects of aging by training to increase strength, flexibility, and suppleness.

CHAPTER 2

Strength, Stretching, and Massage

Weight Training

The fundamental way to replace the loss of strength due to aging is by increasing strength through weight training. You might wonder how weight training can work at all, since we talked in the last chapter about the progressive loss of muscle cells throughout life. Fortunately, there's another side of the story: most muscle cells are never used to their full capacity. Weight training increases the number of muscle fibers that can contract; it also increases the degree to which they contract. Both of these training responses increase the amount of strength available for a given effort. (If you are like most runners, experience may help convince you of the effectiveness of weight training. Runners we train tell us that after a month of weight training, there is no doubt in their minds that they look and feel stronger.)

For masters runners interested in increasing their strength and thereby increasing their racing ability, we will discuss various weight-training equipment and conclude with a weight-training program designed for distance runners (2 miles and beyond).

EQUIPMENT

Free weights is the term usually applied to any variation on barbell/dumbbell equipment — in essence, a pipe with a circular weight at each end. To some extent free weights fell into disuse when more sophisticated (and less dangerous) equipment became available and was purchased by gyms, athletic departments, and professional teams, but free weights do have a number of advantages.

First, they are relatively inexpensive. A beginning set (around 110 pounds) costs less than thirty dollars. Used sets are even cheaper and are widely available in garage sales as New Year's resolutions wane.

Second, free weights work muscle groups in conjunction with each other, instead of isolating a single group in each exercise. While isolation has its advantages, training groups together has benefits too.

There are also drawbacks to using free weights. First, the only thing controlling them is you, and since a weight workout is designed to fatigue the muscles, there may come a time when you have less control over them than you should. Then you can get hurt: a muscle strain, a sprain, even a broken foot if you drop them.

Second, the apparent simplicity of free weights is sometimes deceiving: to be used correctly and safely, free weights often need more equipment than you have available. It may be tempting to use a coffee table for bench presses (lying on your back and pushing the weights straight up from your chest), but coffee tables may collapse from the extra weight and leave you flat on your back, trying to catch a hundred pounds of iron. Even if the table takes the extra strain, consider that you may be too tired to lift the weights the last time and get out from under them. If you're going to do bench presses, use a weight bench.

Third, to be used correctly, free weights require good technique. If you don't know how to bend your knees and get your hips low to pick up a barbell, for example, you could injure your back. So heavy free weights are best used only by people who know what they're doing or by people being watched by an experienced weight coach.

Unless you meet one of the last two requirements, free weights should be kept relatively light — not more than 50 pounds (less if you're small or weak). You can get an excellent workout with free weights of this size; a plus is that high repetitions with less weight produces extra strength with less added muscle bulk and weight — a case of getting stronger while staying light.

Universal systems are characterized by a series of pulleys lifting a stack of weights that slide up and down in an enclosed frame. Instead of adding disks onto the bar, you control the amount of weight by inserting a metal pin at the desired point in the stack. The availability of several different stations around the machine, and several different sets of pulleys, makes it possible for you to exercise a wide variety of muscle groups. The major advantage of this method is that the weights are not free, and even a dropped bar will cause no more than a loud noise (and perhaps a cracked weight). The stations provide some degree of muscle isolation and make it less likely that you will do an exercise "wrong." Universal systems are expensive enough that the best models are found only in gyms and health clubs. (Some smaller home models have appeared recently; if you want the advantages of this type of training at home, be sure to check these for sturdiness and number of stations provided.) The primary drawbacks to universal training are the cost and the lack of adjustability in some systems, which can limit the effectiveness of your training.

The *Nautilus* type of equipment combines the pulley system with a series of cams that vary the resistance of weights in the stack according to the relative strength of the muscle at a given point in its contraction. This, in theory, increases the amount of improvement you can expect from a given workout. Additionally, these machines usually allow a range of adjustment in seat and bench placement so that you can work your muscles through a full range of contraction. The main limitation is that each machine is expensive and is usually designed for only one exercise. A full set of Nautilus-type machinery thus costs a lot of money and will also take up a lot of space.

Which type of equipment should you use? Use what is available. We runners tend to be an introspective, reflective lot. We can spend hours and days debating the relative merits of two different types of running shoes, two different vitamin supplements, two different training schedules. In spite of the fact that running is a very low tech sport, we are always hoping for a high-tech solution, keeping alert to the most recent innovations, looking perhaps for the magic key that will let us run that 5 percent faster we feel is *there*, if we could only get to it.

We sometimes forget that we are more likely to gain that 5 percent if we buy one pair of shoes *or* the other, put them on, and run. The same is true of weights and most other equipment. A week of workouts lifting a portable typewriter in a case will do more for your running than a week of waiting for your new equipment to be delivered. As a practical matter, too, you may have easier access to one type of weight training than another. Finally, *how* you use the weights is more important than whether you have machines or barbells.

TECHNIQUE

Weight-lifting technique can be summarized in a few commonsense rules that will work for you no matter what your ability or strength:

- Warm up and warm down. (Work up a light sweat with mild exercise — calisthenics or stationary bicycle and stretching — before lifting; warm down by stretching.)
- Don't pile on too many weights. (You should be able to do between 8 and 12 repetitions in any exercise, having to work a little on the last two.)
- Don't lift too often. (Total workout time should be about 30–45 minutes no more than three times a week. Allow at least 24 hours between workouts.)
- Don't overspecialize. (Do an exercise for each of the major muscle groups: lower back / buttocks, legs, torso, arms, abdominals.)
- Don't go too fast. (During each repetition, count *two* while lifting the weight, count *four* while letting it go back. Exhale throughout, then inhale moderately before the next repetition.)

The last rule is probably the one most often broken. Too many runners take the term "pumping iron" literally and pump away, no doubt feeling that they're doing more good for themselves by moving the weights quickly — after all, running fast is better training than running slowly, so the same must be true for weights. Besides, it looks a lot more impressive to toss all that mass around. A little reflection may help convince you that it doesn't work that way in weight training. Quick acceleration of the weights uses your fast-twitch muscle fibers, the same ones that give you explosive speed. "Great," you may reply. "I need all the explosive speed I can get." The problem is that the fast-twitch fibers aren't very trainable — that means you can pump iron quickly for a year and not be much better off.

Even worse, once you've accelerated the weights quickly, they tend to complete the exercise on momentum. That means that your slow-twitch muscle fibers — the ones that *are* trainable, and the ones you will use in most of your racing beyond two miles — get an easy ride. So they don't get the full benefit of the workout either.

A little experimentation will probably convince you that it is harder to lift and return weights slowly than to pop them up and down. Additionally, the fibers that are now getting the work are the ones that can benefit

Donald Slocomb, national champion, needs extra strength and flexibility to compete in the steeplechase. (Photograph by Bruce Glikin)

most from your lifting. So if you are going to spend time with weights to help your running, slow down and let them work.

A WEIGHT-LIFTING PROGRAM

Once again, there are a variety of programs available. Most of the good ones use the basic principles outlined above. If you don't have one you like, or don't have one at all, here's one that works:

Warm-up and Stretch: 10 minutes

1. Bench Press	2 sets of 10	Lying on your back on a weight bench, push weights straight up to full arm extension. Return.
2. Pullover	1–2 sets of 10	Lying on your back on the floor or on a weight bench, with weights at arms' length behind your head, bring weights over your head and finish by your sides. Keep arms straight throughout.
3. Lateral Pull-down	2 sets of 10	Usually done on a machine. Reach up and grab bar overhead at almost full arm extension, pull straight down to below chest level.
4. Preacher Curl	2 sets of 10	A curl done at a bench that allows you to rest your upper arms on a padded support and move only your lower arms.
5. Lateral Raises	1 set of 10	Raise dumbbells from your sides to shoulder height; keep wrists and elbows slightly bent.

6. Vertical Hip Lift	2 sets of 20	While holding yourself off the ground with straight arms, either from parallel bars or from a hip lift chair, raise straight legs in front of you to horizontal.
7. Bench Sit-ups	2 sets of 20	Sit-ups lying on an inclined bench; keep knees bent.
8. Back Extensions	1 set of 15	Lying face down with legs secure and hips slightly elevated, move upper torso up from floor to horizontal and return. Do not raise torso higher than hips.

Stretch: 5 minutes

This program is designed to be used during the noncompetitive season, when you are building strength. Once competition starts, it is a good idea to modify, and in some cases eliminate, the weight program, in the same way that you will change your track training as you near the date of your main season.

Circuit Training

Circuit training achieved some popularity among the ranks of elite runners a few years ago, when Sebastian Coe incorporated it in the training that propelled him to the top of the middle-distance running world. Generally speaking, circuit training uses a series of exercises interspersed with running to ensure that the body receives cardiovascular training, strength improvement, and some stretching, all at the same time.

Last year, the Institute for Aerobics Research in Dallas designed a circuit-training program for U.S. Secret Service agents, whose job demands that they be in excellent physical shape but keeps them out of touch with health spas and gyms.

Masters runners often face the same conflict. The following program, therefore, can be used at home or on the road to keep you in good physical condition when you can't do other strength work. The Institute for Aerobics Research recommends that you do each of the following exercises for 30 to 60 seconds and jog in place for 30 to 60 seconds between each exercise. But if you are already keeping to your running schedule, we find that you can eliminate the jogging in between exercises and do the workout solely for its strength and flexibility benefits. For extra strength benefits, the starred exercises (*) may be done with portable ankle and leg weights as you gain proficiency.

1. Push-ups, 30–60 seconds.
2. Leg scissors, 30–60 seconds. Lie on back, legs in air with bent knees. Separate feet horizontally 3–4 feet, then bring them together and cross them, right foot on top. Repeat, with left foot on top. Keep knees above hips to prevent lower back strain.
3. Abdominal curls (sit-ups), 30–60 seconds. Keep feet on floor, knees bent. Curl up, keeping lower back on floor.
4. Arm curls, 30–60 seconds.* The Institute recommends that beginners use 2- to 4-pound weights; intermediates, 4- to 8-pound weights; and experts, 8- to 12-pound weights.
5. Half knee-bends with heel raises, 30–60 seconds. Start with a half-squat (thighs parallel to the floor), then rise up on toes and stand up.
6. Jumping jacks, 30–60 seconds. The old physical-education standby is still a good exercise: feet together, arms at sides; then jump up and land with feet apart, shoulder-width, and hands touching overhead, arms straight. Jump up again and return to starting position. Repeat.
7. Chair dips, 30–60 seconds. Sit in chair, hands on chair arms, legs straight, then scoot forward until you're no longer sitting but are supported only by your arms. Lower and raise yourself by bending and straightening elbows.
8. Side bends, 30–60 seconds.* Stand with arms over head; bend from one side to the other, stretching and strengthening the muscles of the lower sides.
9. "Fire hydrants," 30–60 seconds.* Stand with feet together, swing one leg out to the side, and return. Alternate legs; repeat.
10. Jump rope, 30–60 seconds.
11. Side leg lifts, 30–60 seconds.* Lie on one side; lift top leg as high as comfortable, return. Switch sides. Repeat.
12. Step up and down on stairs or bench, 30–60 seconds.

[Circuit training program used courtesy of the Institute for Aerobics Research, Dallas, Texas.]

Stretching

In *The Self-Coached Runner*, we wrote that stretching was controversial: some runners swore that they couldn't run if they stretched; others swore that they couldn't run if they *didn't*.

In August of 1985 I participated in a high-altitude running camp.* One of my fellow staff members was Bob Anderson, the author of the best-selling book *Stretching*. He agreed, laughing, that stretching was controversial, but he added that, whether it was controversial or not, I would find that I needed to stretch more and more as I aged. Bob was able to convince me of the necessity of beginning a disciplined stretching program on a regular basis to counteract the tightness and inflexibility that I would invariably experience with age and the cumulative rigors of my sport. He added that, unfortunately, there seemed to be a tendency among masters runners to stretch less as they grew older, the opposite of what they should do.

Accordingly, we include here two stretching routines. The first routine is designed for use before and after training and racing. The second routine can provide additional benefits when used during a runner's leisure time. Neither routine takes more than fifteen minutes, but they will help the masters runner avoid pain, soreness, and injury, all of which increase with age.

With any stretching routine, there are a number of general tips you should follow to avoid feeling worse rather than better. The basic rules are: *relax, go slow, don't bounce,* and *avoid pain.*

- Relax your body and your mind before and during stretching.
- Exhale while first getting into position to do a stretch.
- Gently ease into each stretch until you feel the beginning of tension in the target muscle group.
- Ease deeper into the stretch as you feel the muscle group relaxing.
- Decrease the intensity of the stretch if pain occurs.

---

* Throughout the book, "we" and "our" refer to both authors, "I" and "my" to Allan Lawrence.

Figure 1. The Calf Stretch   *Figure 2. The Ankle-Foot Stretch*

Figure 3. The Calf-Hamstring-Shoulder   *Figure 4. The Quadriceps*
Combo Stretch   *Stretch*

(Photographs of figures 1–24 by Bruce Glikin)

- Hold each stretch for 2 to 6 breathing cycles (5 seconds inhale + 5 seconds exhale = one cycle).
- If one side of the body is tighter than the other, hold the stretch on the stiffer side a little longer to equalize muscle flexibility.
- Ease gently out of the stretching position after the stretch has been completed.
- Do not become discouraged if you cannot do all the stretches properly at first. It took you years to stiffen up, and it will take time to reverse the process.
- Be especially careful with stretches that require joints to be bent acutely (such as the Hurdler's Stretch), and make sure that you keep your back straight when stretching.

For additional information on stretching, the authors recommend *Stretching*, by Bob Anderson (Bolinas, California: Shelter Publications, 1980).

BASIC STRETCHES BEFORE TRAINING AND COMPETITION

The Calf Stretch (Figure 1)
Face a tree, wall, or similar vertical support surface. Stand a short distance away from it and place your hands on the support. (As an alternative position, you may place your forearms on the support surface with your forehead resting on the back of your hands.) Shift your weight to one leg by stepping forward and slightly bending the other knee. With your back leg straight and your heel flat on the ground, move your hips forward. Both feet should be pointed straight ahead. Hold the stretch for about 25 seconds, and then stretch the other leg. Repeat the procedure until both calves have been stretched 3 times.

The Ankle-Foot Stretch (Figure 2)
(This stretches the Achilles tendon and the bottom of the foot.)
After completing the Calf Stretch, move one leg forward, knee bent, for support. Roll up on the ball of your back foot, bending your knee slightly, and rock your foot gently in a side-to-side movement, making sure to stretch your toes and ankle. Hold for 10 to 15 seconds. Repeat with the other leg.

The Calf-Hamstring-Shoulder Combo Stretch (Figure 3)
(This stretches the calf of one leg, the hamstring of the opposite leg, and both shoulders.)

Figure 5. The Hamstring and Lower Back Stretch (Version 1)

Figure 6. The Hamstring and Lower Back Stretch (Version 2)

Figure 7. The Hamstring and Lower Back Stretch (Version 3)

Stand about 18 inches from a wall (or other support), facing it. Place your hands on the wall and step backward with one leg, planting your foot flat on the ground. Straighten both legs and bend at the waist until your back is parallel with the ground. Hold this position for 10 to 20 seconds. Repeat this procedure with the other leg. (Use this stretch in series with the Calf Stretch and the Ankle-Foot Stretch.)

The Quadriceps (front of the thigh) Stretch (Figure 4)

Facing a vertical support (about 18 inches away), put your hand flat against it, then stand on your right leg and bring your left foot up behind you, catching it with your left hand. Pull your foot upward gently, keeping your back straight. Hold this position for about 25 seconds. Stretch the other leg the same way. Repeat until both legs have been stretched 3 times.

The Hamstring and Lower Back Stretch (Figures 5, 6, 7)

(The hamstrings are the long parallel muscles that run down the backs of your thighs.)

There are several versions of this stretch:

Version 1 (Figure 5) Stand upright and place your feet 36 to 48 inches apart, toes pointing forward. Keeping both legs straight (knees bent only slightly), lean forward from the hips. Place your left hand in front of your right foot, and stretch your right arm behind your back, resting your hand on your left hip. Hold the stretch for 10 to 25 seconds before returning to an upright position. Repeat the stretch on the opposite side. Repeat until both sides have been stretched 3 times.

Version 2 (Figure 6) Stand upright with your feet approximately 18 to 36 inches apart, toes pointed straight ahead. (As you become more flexible, you may move your feet closer together.) Bend forward from your hips, keeping your back straight (you may bend your knees slightly if necessary). Stretch both hands out in front of your feet and then back to touch your toes. Hold the stretch for 10 to 25 seconds before returning to an upright position. Repeat 2 more times.

Version 3 (Figure 7) This stretch is similar to version 2, except one leg is crossed over the other at the shins and ankles.

Figure 8. The Groin Stretch
(Version 1)

Figure 9. The Groin Stretch
(Version 2)

The Groin Stretch (Figures 8, 9)
Sit comfortably on the floor. Put the soles of your feet together, holding them in place with both hands. Using this starting position there are two versions of the stretch:

Version 1 (Figure 8) Keeping your back straight, pull your toes back toward your groin. Try to keep your knees flat on the floor. Hold the stretch comfortably for 10 to 20 seconds. Ease slowly out of the stretch. Repeat once more.

Version 2 (Figure 9) From the same starting position, pull your upper body forward from the hips, keeping your back straight and your elbows outside your legs. Hold for 10 to 20 seconds. Ease gently out of the stretch. Repeat once more.

The Modified "Lunge" Stretch (Figure 10)
(This stretch benefits the lower abdomen, quadriceps, and hips.)

Holding your upper body upright, take a long step forward, moving slowly into a "lunge" position, pointing straight ahead. Keep your front leg bent at about 90 degrees, using your arms for support. Hold the stretch for 10 to 20 seconds. Repeat, using your other leg.

Figure 10. The Modified "Lunge" Stretch

Figure 11. The Horizontal Elongation Stretch

Figure 12. The Horizontal Elongation Stretch (Variation)

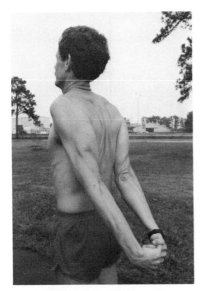

Figure 13. Neck and Shoulder Stretch (Version 1)

Figure 14. Neck and Shoulder Stretch (Version 2)

The Horizontal Elongation Stretch (Figure 11)
(Benefits feet, ankles, legs, abdomen, chest, and back.)
Lie flat on the floor. Extend your arms over your head and stretch your fingers straight. Stretch your legs as far as you can in the opposite direction and point your toes. Hold for 3 to 5 seconds, then relax. Repeat 2 or 3 times. (As a variation, tuck in your abdomen as you stretch.)

Horizontal Elongation Stretch (Variation) (Figure 12)
(This variation benefits the muscles in the hip area.)
Starting from the position above, raise and bend your left knee, pulling it to your chest. Hold the stretch for 25 seconds, keeping your shoulder and head flat on the floor. Repeat with the opposite leg.

Neck and Shoulder Stretch (Figures 13, 14)

Version 1 (Figure 13) Stand upright and place both arms behind your back. Lock your arms by interlacing your fingers. Rotate your elbows *inward* as you slowly straighten your arms. Hold the stretch for 5 to 15 seconds. Repeat 2 more times.

Version 2 (Figure 14) From the starting position of version 1, lift your arms out and up from your back until you feel a comfortable stretch in your upper arms and shoulders. Hold the stretch for 5 to 15 seconds. Repeat stretch 2 more times.

The Hurdler's Stretch (Figure 15)
(This stretch benefits the hamstrings, quadriceps, and adductors, the muscles along the insides of your thighs.)
Sit on the floor. Move your left leg out in front of your body. Position your right leg (bent at the knee with your foot behind your leg, toes pointing out) as close to 90 degrees from your body as possible. Keeping your back straight, move your upper body forward until your chest is over your extended left leg. (For reference, look at a photograph of a hurdler clearing a hurdle.) Reach toward your left foot with both hands. Hold the stretch for 10 to 25 seconds, then straighten up. (At this point you may lean backward and hold for 10 to 25 seconds.) Change legs and repeat the stretch.

Figure 15. The Hurdler's Stretch

Figure 16. The "Texas Cow Rail" Stretch

ADVANCED LEISURE STRETCHING

As you become more accustomed to and comfortable with a regular stretching routine, you may wish to add to the basic stretches you have mastered. We include below some stretches for this purpose.

Always keep in mind that your stretching activities are specifically designed to reduce muscle tension, preserve and increase body flexibility, and prevent injuries. But remember above all that stretching is not an unpleasant medicine that you have to force down in order to stay healthy. Stretching is "good" for you because the body needs to stretch; if you're doing it right, it should feel good.

The "Texas Cow Rail" Stretch (Figure 16)
(This stretch benefits an often-overlooked area of the body: the rotator muscles, small muscles in the buttocks that provide stability to the hips and are responsible for proper tracking of the feet. Tight rotators make the feet turn out during walking and running.)

Find a hip-high, level, horizontal support, and rest the outside of the calf and the foot on it. Bend forward from the hips, keeping your head erect. Try to touch your shoulder to your knee. Hold the stretch for 10 to 25 seconds. Repeat the stretch with the other leg.

Upper Back and Hamstring Stretch (Figures 17, 18)

Version 1 Begin this stretch in a sitting position. Roll back onto your shoulders and thrust your feet and legs into a vertical position. Use both arms to support your hips (elbows and upper arms flat on the floor). Stretch your toes toward the sky. Hold the stretch for 10 to 20 seconds.

Version 2 Beginning with the final position of version 1, lower your legs until they approach or touch the ground behind your head. Hold this position for 5 to 10 seconds before returning your legs to vertical. Repeat the stretch 2 more times.

Hamstring and Lower Back Stretch (Figure 19)
Begin in a sitting position. Straighten your left leg and place the sole of your right foot against the inside of your left knee. Bend slowly forward from the hips, keeping your back straight, and allowing your left knee to bend slightly. Grasp your left ankle or touch your left toes with

Figure 17. Upper Back and Hamstring Stretch (Version 1)

Figure 18. Upper Back and Hamstring Stretch (Version 2)

Figure 19. Hamstring and Lower Back Stretch

Figure 20. Inside Thigh and Hip Stretch

both hands. Hold for 10 to 20 seconds. Repeat the stretch with the opposite leg.

Inside Thigh and Hip Stretch (Figure 20)
Begin this stretch standing with legs wide apart and both feet pointing forward. Turn your left foot outward, bending your leg at the knee and sliding your foot back until your left thigh is almost parallel to the ground. Use your arms for support. Place your left hand on the ground slightly in front of your left foot. Place your right hand slightly behind your left hand, parallel with your bent right leg. Hold the stretch for 10 to 20 seconds. Repeat the stretch with your other leg.

Hips, Lower Back, and Chest Stretch (Figure 21)
Lie on your back and roll onto your left hip, bending your right knee approximately 90 degrees. Place your right foot on top of your left knee, using your left hand to hold your right knee flat on the ground. Move your right arm out 90 degrees from your body. Rotate your right arm and lean backward until your shoulders and right arm are flat on the ground. Hold the stretch for 10 to 20 seconds. Return to starting position and repeat the stretch on the other side.

Hamstring and Hip Stretch (Figure 22)
Lie on the floor with both legs stretched straight. Bend your right knee as you reach forward and grasp your right ankle with your left hand. Place your right hand and forearm around your bent right knee. Pull your right leg toward your chest, keeping your head and shoulders on the floor. Hold for 10 to 20 seconds. Repeat the stretch with your left leg.

Kneeling Hamstring Stretch (Figure 23)
(In this stretch the hamstrings are stretched equally, with less stress on the lower back than in the standing position.)

Start in a kneeling position, with your hands on the ground in front of you. Move one leg out to the side and straighten it, toes pointing up. Using your hands for balance, turn your body toward your outstretched leg. Hold this position for 10 to 20 seconds. Repeat the stretch with the other leg.

Sitting Hip Stretch (Figure 24)
(This is a beneficial stretch for the prevention of "ilio-tibial band syndrome," an overuse injury that causes pain along the outside of the knee.)

Figure 21. Hips, Lower Back, and Chest Stretch

Figure 22. Hamstring and Hip Stretch

Figure 23. Kneeling Hamstring Stretch

Figure 24. Sitting Hip Stretch

Starting in a sitting position, pull one foot then the other toward your groin. Twist your body slowly to the right, bending at the waist toward your knee. Stretch both arms out in front of you, placing them on the floor, while keeping your right knee flat. (Placing light weights on the knee may be beneficial.) Hold the position for 10 to 20 seconds. Repeat the stretch with your body twisted to the left side.

Massage

"Massage can bind a joint that is too loose and loosen a joint that is too tight."

— Hippocrates, 380 B.C.

Although it is one of the oldest of all the sports-related therapy systems, predating even stretching as an organized activity relating to sports activity, massage has had a checkered career. Although at times it has received its due as a useful tool in physical therapy, it has also been called (by those who have misunderstood its role) a "lazy man's exercise." In recent years, sports massage has gained acceptance as a preventive and rehabilitative tool in sports medicine. Massage therapists are licensed in most states and are trained in anatomy, physiology, and kinesiology. Much of their training is "hands-on" practice under the supervision of competent and qualified teachers.

BENEFITS OF MASSAGE

There are several benefits that the over-35 runner may derive from massage:

- It speeds up the unloading of wastes through the lymphatic channels.
- It assists in breaking down adhesions and freeing scar tissue after injury.
- It helps overcome tightness in tendons and ligaments.
- It can help prevent injury by the combination of the effects listed above.

- Finally, it produces a sedative effect on the muscles, offsetting to some extent the "on-edge" feeling frequently associated with heavy training.

MASSAGE TECHNIQUES

If you've ever seen any old boxing movies, your impression of massage is probably influenced somewhat by the image of a middle-aged man chewing a cigar and giving advice while he pummels the body of his hapless victim. But the percussion movements you see in old movies are no longer used; tapping, slapping, and beating the body to stimulate muscles and superficial nerves is now held to be too harmful a practice unless the therapist is extremely experienced. Professional massage therapists are currently trained in a number of techniques, or "movements," that are used in basic sports massage: squeezing or compression, kneading, and friction.

There is no doubt that you will get maximum benefits from sports massage when it is performed by an experienced practitioner. There are, however, a number of massage techniques a self-coached runner can use on his or her own muscles with beneficial results. One happy consequence of being runners is that the muscles we tend to strain and overuse are in our legs, so that they are easy for us to work on ourselves. Imagine a swimmer trying to give himself a massage.

Here are some basic techniques you can apply to yourself that will produce good results.

Direct pressure is probably the simplest to understand and use, and it may be the most beneficial. To use the direct pressure technique, first pick a spot on a muscle or a tendon you think could benefit from loosening up. Put one thumb on the spot, then put the other thumb on top of the first thumb. Press in on the spot fairly hard (as hard as you can without causing pain) and hold for a count of 20. Move one thumb's width up (toward the heart) and repeat.

Having the massage move from the distal part of a leg toward the heart ensures that any waste products freed or generated by the massage process will be moved in the same direction that the blood and lymphatic system is already moving.

A few attempts at spot massage will convince you that (even though it works and feels good) it is time-consuming. The following techniques are a little faster, but (in our opinion) not as effective:

Transverse massage. Pick a spot on one side of a muscle or tendon and press down. While maintaining pressure, slide your thumb across the muscle, finishing on the opposite side from which you started. Go back to the same side, pick a spot a little higher, and repeat. Continue until the entire muscle has been massaged.

Longitudinal massage. Using one or more fingers, press down on a wide strip at the far end (away from the heart) of a muscle or tendon. Then, maintaining pressure, slide up the muscle or tendon, "milking" and squeezing it as you go.

MASSAGE AND INJURY

Never massage an injury site until at least 48 hours have passed since the injury was sustained. In most injuries to which runners fall victim, there is an immediate release of blood and lymph fluid around the injury site. Any direct-site physical treatment, particularly massage, is likely to increase the damage.

On the other hand, you must be careful not to delay too long: if you do, muscle wasting and atrophy may occur, and scar tissue (or adhesions) may develop. Massage therapy for injuries works best when combined with other traditional forms of injury treatment such as ice-cold compresses, rest, and elevation. It can also be combined with electrical stimulation, ultrasound and shortwave treatments, and anti-inflammatory drugs.

But massage is best used to help prevent injuries in the first place, either through a competent therapist or through your own massage therapy. Additionally, the over-35 runner will find that sports massage can help to improve muscle strength and flexibility and, through increased circulation, can lead to the ability to perform both anaerobic and aerobic work more efficiently. All of these add up to better racing.

CHAPTER 3

Nutrition and Diet

DIETS FOR RUNNERS are a lot like today's running shoes: there are many varieties and brands available that fit the special requirements of this segment or that segment of the market, but there is no "universal" shoe or diet that exactly fits everyone. However, just as we now know a lot more about the qualities of a "good" running shoe than we did twenty years ago, so with diets: our level of nutritional knowledge is so much better than it was only a few years ago that we can now provide general diet guidelines, within which almost anyone can find a diet that will improve health and increase performance. Such guidelines are the topic of this chapter.

Diet Fads

In *The Self-Coached Runner II*, we wrote that runners tend to seek high-tech solutions to low-tech problems. That tendency is nowhere more evident than in the field of nutrition. Largely in vain, runners have sought significant benefits from bee pollen, carbohydrate loading, protein loading, large doses of various vitamins and minerals, and combinations of these or other foods in "magic" diets guaranteed to let you lose weight, lower your cholesterol, and qualify for the Olympics.

Just as fast as runners have been encouraged to adopt various foods as performance panaceas, the general public has been exposed to a series of diet fads that *exclude* one food after another. Typically, a hot new diet receives a lot of its national attention by discovering that one or more foods, hitherto accepted as safe, are in fact "killers" lurking in the human food chain. Such has been the fate, recently, of red meat, dairy products, and eggs.

Usually the American public does a pretty good job of shunning a food that makes the national media "blacklist." Curiously, and unfortunately, however, the public is much less successful at replacing a "bad" food with another, better, food from the same food group. Thus the decrease in beef, dairy product, and egg consumption was not matched by an increase in the consumption of fish or chicken. Instead, sales of candy and snack items boomed, indicating that Americans were trading a known source of high dietary cholesterol for food items that had equally dangerous (although not as well publicized) highly saturated fats, besides being much lower in protein, vitamins, and minerals, and much higher in salt and sugar, than the foods they replaced.

One final by-product of recent nutrition research has been some uncertainty on the part of the public as to what's "true," as onetime villains in the food lineup have been reappraised. Recently, for instance, research has established that the fat and cholesterol in beef was not as instrumental in raising human cholesterol as was first thought. Eggs ("bad guys" for the last thirty years) were found to have lower levels of cholesterol than scientists had initially reported, and the American Heart Association responded by stating that people with no known cholesterol problems could eat as many as four eggs a week without effect. One type of fatty acid from cold-water fish was even found to be *helpful* in lowering serum cholesterol levels in humans. As a result of these changes, some members of the public seem to think, incorrectly, that "nutritionists can't make up their minds," or "no one really knows what helps or hurts."

Nothing could be further from the truth. The facts about the effects of diet on the human organism are better known today than at any time in history. Furthermore, despite the dozens of diet books, calorie counters, nutritional supplements, and fad foods common to modern society, the basic principles of good nutrition are neither difficult to understand nor to apply.

Common Knowledge and Common Sense

As is true of nearly every problem area of training and racing, most of the questions about a good diet for runners can be answered with a combination of common knowledge and common sense. The "common knowledge" about diet comes from a wide variety of sources, including a number of books and articles by nutritionists, advice from physicians, and recommendations from national health-care bodies such as the American Heart Association and the National Research Council of the National Science Foundation. We call it "common knowledge" because all these different individuals and groups are in essential agreement. Here is what they agree on:

The composition of your diet should be about 15 percent protein, 30 percent (or less) fat, and from 55 to 60 percent carbohydrates for the general adult population (60 to 70 percent carbohydrates for endurance runners). Additional considerations are as follows:

Protein, found in meats, dairy products, and eggs (where it is usually associated with fats and cholesterol), is also available in smaller amounts in grains and legumes (peas and beans). The typical American diet contains a good deal more than 15 percent protein. Excess protein is stored as body fat and is also dehydrating both because the process of digesting protein is water-intensive and because the waste products of protein digestion must be excreted.

Your diet's maximum 30 percent *fat* calories should be further limited as follows (and if you have a cholesterol problem — yes, even good runners can have one — you will probably need to cut fats even more):

- 10 percent or less of your total calories should be saturated fats (lard, beef fat, tropical oils, hydrogenated vegetable oils).
- The remainder should be polyunsaturated and (probably better) monounsaturated fats (olive oil, peanut oil) and cold-water fish oils (tuna, salmon, herring, and shrimp).

Carbohydrates in your diet should be mostly complex carbohydrates (found in grains, vegetables, fruits, and pasta), since the sources of most complex carbohydrates also offer the most vitamins, minerals, and fiber. Limit simple carbohydrates (sugars) to 10 percent of your caloric intake.

Fiber is an important (and, lately, widely publicized) ingredient in a healthy diet. Although, unlike protein, fats, and carbohydrates, it plays no direct role in physical fitness, it reduces blood cholesterol and may lower your risk of colon cancer. A diet with the recommended percentage of 60 to 70 percent carbohydrates will usually have, as an additional benefit, a high level of dietary fiber.

With proper attention to nutrition and diet, Thomas Waterhouse was able to drop 30 pounds and run a 2:54 marathon. (Photograph by Bruce Glikin)

Vitamins and minerals are found in nearly all fresh foods. There is still little evidence that athletes need higher levels of vitamins than a well-balanced diet provides, but most athletes take a vitamin-mineral supplement. Actually, athletes do need more minerals, because they use more (with their higher metabolic rates) and lose more (in perspiration) than sedentary people do. Women need to be especially careful to maintain adequate iron intake because they lose iron through menstruation. Mega-doses of either vitamins or minerals can be dangerous and should be avoided.

Water, according to nutritionist Lori Valencic, is the nutrient most neglected by athletes. It is vital for temperature control and metabolic processes. Dehydration can be caused by both low water intake and overuse of diuretics such as caffeine and alcohol.

Special Requirements: Weight Loss

If you are a runner and feel the need to diet, it is probably because you are overweight. "Overweight" for runners, however, doesn't always have the same meaning as it does for the general population. A substantial proportion of the American public is ten to fifteen pounds overweight and is apparently content to remain so. To a runner, an extra ten pounds can feel like thirty if your legs have to carry it over the last mile of a 10K, and an extra fifteen pounds may simply make it impossible to train for and run a marathon.

On the other hand, as a runner you have advantages over the general public. Research has shown that fat rats that were given diets but no exercise lost weight but did not lower their percentage of body fat — that is, as Jane Brody puts it, they went from being big fat rats to little fat rats. Combining exercise with diet lets you lose weight *and* lower the amount of fat in your body.

If you need to lose weight, keep these commonsense rules in mind:

- "Quick fix" diets usually don't work — the "crash" weight loss is more than compensated for by the body's "rebound" tendency. (The one time a "quick fix" diet may be a good idea is when you need to convince yourself that you *can* in fact lose weight. Even then, you should abandon the quick diet as soon as you've lost a

few pounds in favor of a more gradual and nutritionally sound one.)
· Maintain your normal training program as you gradually reduce your caloric intake.
· As the fatty deposits in your body shrink and are replaced by muscle, your body weight might remain the same or even rise (muscle fiber weighs more than fat).
· You probably did not gain your extra weight overnight, so don't expect to lose it overnight.
· Remember that you possess a unique body physiology, so some dietary methods that work well for others may not work for you.

Special Requirements: Training and Competition

The diet you should eat to help you compete is the one given above — there *aren't* any magic diets! However, the diet outlined above *will* do a lot for your ability to train and compete. Here's why:

First, it provides a lot of complex carbohydrates, which your body uses as the primary source of energy when you're exercising hard. As a bonus, carbohydrates (at only 4 calories per gram, the same as proteins) allow runners to eat a lot to satisfy their distance-training hunger without incurring too high a calorie penalty.

Second, it provides enough protein to allow the body to build and replace muscle tissue needed and used in training and racing. But it does not include a lot of extra protein that the body has to convert to fat or to use, inefficiently, as fuel.

Third, it provides enough vitamins and minerals for the body to perform efficiently both in the metabolic processes that provide energy and in the use of energy in the muscles.

Finally — and probably most important to the masters runner — it limits your intake of fats. Some fat in the diet is vital to the body: fats contain trace elements and are a tremendous source of energy (9 calories per gram), which your body needs whenever you exercise longer than 90 minutes. But fats have a bad name, and deservedly so: besides their contribution to America's obesity (and its attendant health problems), they are largely responsible for high cholesterol levels in the blood, causing — in addition to an increased likelihood of heart attacks and strokes — restriction of blood flow to the heart, lungs, and muscles, lowering cardiovascular efficiency and muscle power, and making you run slower.

But, to paraphrase a slogan, fats don't kill people, or even make them slow down. People do it to themselves, by not watching their diet. Worst of all, people don't watch their diet even though it's not hard to do.

In line with our dietary philosophy of "common knowledge and common sense," we include here a sample one-day's food plan of a male runner, about 140 pounds, who's training about 40 miles a week. The standard daily caloric intake for an adult male is about 1,700 calories, and, as a rule of thumb, you can add about 100 calories extra to your diet for each mile you run. He's averaging a little under 6 miles a day, so he should eat about 2,200 calories a day to maintain his current weight. Here's how he might do it, keeping to the percentages outlined in the first part of this chapter:

Breakfast

½ grapefruit
1 cup bran cereal or oatmeal
1 cup skimmed milk

Lunch

2 tuna sandwiches (made with water-packed tuna, imitation mayonnaise, and lettuce and tomato if desired)
1 cup raw vegetables (carrots or broccoli)
1 apple, pear, or orange
1 cup skimmed milk

Dinner

1 four-ounce chicken breast (skinned), broiled or grilled, with herbs and lemon slice
1 baked potato
2 dinner rolls
1 fruit or green vegetable
1 cup skimmed milk

Snacks

3 graham crackers spread with peanut butter
3 cups popcorn
1 fruit

Most of the obvious fat in this runner's meals comes from the meat (about 8 grams) and from the peanut butter (about 24 grams). There is some fat in a number of other items as well, but these are the main sources. The fat in the meat and the peanut butter adds up to 286 calories, or about 13 percent of his daily caloric intake. *But* this number could double (or more) depending on how much vegetable oil (at 5–14 grams of fat per tablespoon) is used in the mayonnaise in his tuna sandwiches, and what he puts on his popcorn, his dinner rolls, and his baked potato.

RECOMMENDED FOR FURTHER READING

This book is not designed to be a diet or recipe book. If you would like to find out more about nutrition and recipes that use the "common knowledge and commonsense" diet approach, we recommend these books:

Kenneth Cooper, *Controlling Cholesterol* (New York: Bantam, 1988).
Jane Brody, *Jane Brody's Good Food Book* (New York: Norton, 1985).

CHAPTER 4

Sports Psychology

> "Two runners stand side by side at the starting line of a race. Both have equal ability, equal training, and equal desire to run well. One will cross the finish line before the other. Why?"
> — Frances Baxter, M.S.W.

ALTHOUGH THE SCIENCE of sports psychology is growing rapidly, in the minds of many people it is a discipline designed exclusively to assist the elite athlete rather than the mainstream competitor. There is, however, growing recognition that sports psychology techniques can bring many kinds of benefits to the mid-range athlete — and, in particular, to runners over 35.

Most of the advances in mental training for sports can be credited to Soviet and East German sports psychologists, who began wide-scale research with substantial government encouragement and funding in the mid-1950s. The results quickly became obvious, as these nations — neither of which had a great sports tradition at the time — became, almost overnight, major players on the international sports scene.

The first benefit modern sports psychology offers is the destruction of old locker-room myths about the psychological aspects of competition. For example, old misconceptions about "mental toughness" ("some have it; some don't") are being replaced by the knowledge that competitiveness can be learned in disciplined and structured systems of self-help programs combined with professional guidance. Even more important, recent developments in sports psychology have demonstrated that one of the major errors of American coaching has been to concentrate on the elimination or correction of specific faults. The current emphasis is on the athlete's development of goal-directed confidence and positive mental preparation for training and competition.

WHO CAN BENEFIT FROM SPORTS PSYCHOLOGY?

If you enjoy competition and wish to improve your competitive skills, how would you answer these questions?

- In competition, do you become "psyched up" or "psyched out"?
- Can you relax?
- Do you worry a lot about your training and your ability to compete?
- Do you have difficulty sleeping before competition?
- Do you think a lot about probable failure, or negative consequences, in upcoming races?
- Do you expect to be successful when you work diligently toward a reasonable goal?
- Do you become embarrassed, self-conscious, or surprised when you are successful?
- Do you expect to be successful?
- When you succeed, do you attribute your success to your own hard work, natural skill, superior competitive effort, etc., or do you attribute it to luck, favorable conditions, or someone else (coach, partner, parent, spouse)?
- Are you reaching toward success or running from failure?

If your answer to any of these questions indicates a lack of competitive confidence, you can benefit from practicing and mastering the mental preparation skills discussed in this chapter.

Mental Training

In *The Self-Coached Runner*, I referred to a post-marathon emotional and mental letdown that many runners experienced. I labeled this condition the "Battered Mind Syndrome." In the six years since the publication of that book, I have seen a similar type of malady affect a lot of runners — not only marathoners — at a variety of points in their training, not just after a race. This problem did not seem to correlate with a runner's ability, age, sex, or years of running experience. The frequent occurrence of this condition bothered me because, after all, running was supposed to *improve* the quality of a runner's life. In these instances, however, it was doing the reverse.

Trying to discover the causes of this problem, and in hopes of finding some cure, I looked into current research in this area. Fortunately, I was coaching a professional sports psychologist, Kirk Coverstone, and a social worker, Frances Baxter, at the time. Their encouragement and knowledge have been of significant benefit in writing this chapter.

Since the publication of *The Self-Coached Runner,* our knowledge of the mental aspects of competitive running has undergone dramatic changes. The following principles have emerged:

- Mental toughness can be developed by working on specific mental training techniques.
- Seemingly insignificant factors can, in combination, seriously affect your ability to train and to compete.
- "Performance inhibiting factors" ("PIFs" to the sports psychologist) can be identified and overcome.
- There is a "spin-off" from mental training in sports that will improve creativity and productivity in other areas of endeavor.
- Adjustments can be made to your training level while you work to alleviate or eliminate PIFs.

Many of the factors that may be limiting your ability to race and to train can be identified by using the self-administered stress test at the end of this chapter. Once these factors are identified, you can modify your training according to the suggestions included here, as you work to reduce the stresses affecting your training.

FEAR OF FAILURE: ONE ATHLETE'S STORY

Kirk Coverstone, Ph.D., sports psychologist, works with a variety of athletes in many different sports. He specializes in counseling athletes in the use of mental preparation techniques and in handling competitive stress. He is in a unique position to do so because his own sports experience is representative of the large percentage of athletes who drop out of their sport with the feeling that they have failed.

A promising athlete in high school, Kirk breezed through his sophomore and junior years in track and cross-country competition with a relative lack of pressure. The problems began in his senior year, when the expectations of his coach and his teammates were much higher.

"You've got to run well," they told him. "If *you* don't win, *we* can't win!"

Kirk Coverstone concentrates on relaxing while running up Heartbreak Hill, Boston.

Kirk recalls: "I began to struggle with the whole issue of the fear of failure. When I failed to reach a goal that was expected of me, I experienced deep dejection. Even if I reached my goal, it was only a temporary relief, a fleeting sense of accomplishment. I was always asking myself, 'Can I repeat?' My whole sense of well-being hinged on my running performance."

When Kirk finished high school, he enrolled at a university noted for its top track teams and became a "walk-on" — a nonscholarship member of the track team. But even the lack of scholarship pressure didn't ease the internal pressure he put on himself.

"In college I developed a policy of taking no risks. I had the philosophy, If you don't try, you can't really fail! But naturally, I couldn't succeed either!

"I dropped off the team after my sophomore year, and for the next twelve years I could only think about what *could* have been and what I *might* have done."

In 1982, Kirk Coverstone, by then a practicing clinical psychologist, began competitive running again.

"I loved getting back into competition, and I was looking for a personal best in every race. Nevertheless, I still had the underlying belief that if I really tried and then failed, it would be terrible! Accordingly, after every race, I still had that old characteristic thought: Imagine what I could have done if I had trained properly."

Early in 1985 I became acquainted with Kirk and soon began supervising his training. We had many "talk and thought" sessions in which we discussed the entire area of "competitive hang-up." We both concluded that Kirk was missing an essential element in his mental approach to competition: a commitment to "put it on the line" without any form of mental reservation. Kirk identifies this period as the turning point of his running career, the time when he finally came to grips with the idea of reaching toward success rather than running from failure.

Using himself as a test subject, Kirk began working on a system of relaxation techniques, imagery, and self-suggestion. By combining his own competitive experience with his specialized training, he was able to develop an effective range of treatments for a variety of athletes from different sports who suffer from a multitude of performance-inhibiting problems.

Additionally, Kirk's own recent competitive results have been impressive: back-to-back PR's in the Boston Marathon, combined with a relaxed

"Pat" Patrick, professional counselor, used goal setting to break 4 hours in the marathon. (Photograph by Bruce Glikin)

confidence in his running and a general improvement in the quality of his life.

SETTING MENTAL ASSISTANCE GOALS

In *The Self-Coached Runner,* we set out a number of training and competitive principles for the self-coached runner. Those given on the following pages supplement the advice offered in our earlier book. As has been our practice in writing books for runners who coach themselves, we present recent applications of sports psychology in a series of step-by-step exercises that allow the individual runner to incorporate the principles of sports psychology into his or her own training and racing.

Goal Setting

The principle of goal setting is certainly not new to distance running; it goes back at least to 490 B.C., when Pheidippides decided he was going to run to Athens. What is new is the degree of sophistication in mental goal-setting techniques.

In setting normal goals, the most important point is to set goals that are "realistic" in terms of your ability. To this principle, you should add the further concepts of "subjective" and "objective" goals. As used here, *objective* goals are entirely within your power to achieve. An example might be, "I need to run 50 miles weekly in training and break 38 minutes for 10K." *Subjective* goals are in part under your control, but they are also dependent upon the performances of others — for example, "I would like to finish in the top 10 percent of my age group in my next 10K race." Obviously, if you plan on setting a subjective goal, you need to do so very carefully to ensure that you are not setting yourself up for failure at the same time.

The other important general rule to remember is: Keep your goal statements positive ("I will relax" rather than "I won't tie up"). Negative statements reinforce an undesired outcome.

GOAL-SETTING STRATEGY

When you're outlining your goals in running-related activities, you should try to set a *range* of goals, because doing so allows you to provide for a range of possible outcomes in your race, *each of which is to some degree a success*. Mental preparation of this type not only more realistically reflects the actual variation in performance most racers experience, but also has the beneficial result of making your race no longer a black-or-white affair (either "I made my time" or "I blew it"). Goal setting should usually include the following range of possible outcomes:

- *Dream goal*. This is your vision of the best of all possible outcomes, assuming ideal conditions and peak mental and physical performance on your part. (Note that the description says "the best of all *possible* outcomes." Even a dream goal should be within your possible range, so don't list "breaking the world record" unless you're really that good. Just try to decide what you could really do if you had one of those "once in a lifetime" races.)
- *Excellent performance*. A race outcome with which you'd be very happy — perhaps a PR for the distance or on that particular course, if you're ready to run a PR. On the other hand, an "excellent performance" might be much slower than your PR if you are coming back from an injury or illness.
- *Good performance*. A highly satisfying competitive performance, but not one that really surprises you.
- *Fair performance*. One with which you're satisfied and moderately pleased.
- *Acceptable performance*. One that meets your standards as set by the statement "I should run at least _____ in this race," when the blank space is filled in with a time that seems easily attainable.

Remember that these goals should be objective and verifiable in competitive situations and should not be based on factors beyond your control, such as the performance of others.

USING SUBGOALS

It's usually a good idea to establish subgoals for your racing and training efforts, both as a way to establish a yardstick for your performance during the race itself and as insurance against the effect of a poor race on your mental preparation for future races.

Most runners are familiar with one type of subgoal, the time "split" you get at the end of every mile in most races. By knowing the average mile pace needed to finish the race in the required time, a runner can tell easily whether he or she is "on pace."

Other subgoals are not used as often but can be just as helpful. If you've had trouble in the past holding a pace that you should be able to maintain, set a subgoal like "I will run the last mile in under 7 minutes." Then, no matter how bad or good your race is going before, you have a challenge that will help keep your mind on the race. And, if you're having a bad day and running really poorly, achieving your subgoal in the last mile split may be the only bright spot in the race — and may make the difference between telling yourself "I was out of it from the beginning" and "Even when I'm having an off day, I can still finish strong."

WRITE IT DOWN

We recommend that once a runner has established training and competition goals and subgoals for herself, she should set them down in writing. We feel this step is essential, because the act of writing establishes a commitment far more binding than mere mental intention. In addition, we suggest that you go beyond the limitations of a running schedule to develop a "Performance Training Guide."

Such a guide differs from the normal training schedule in that it includes personal objectives that can directly influence your running, as well as training objectives relating to your personal training sessions. *Personal objectives* might include such matters as gradual dietary change, weight reduction, cross-training, stretching, warm-up and warm down procedures, and so forth. *Training objectives* could be taken from any of the schedules in this book, with or without modification.

Such a training guide should include both long-term and short-term goals. For most of us, it's easier to imagine doing "what's right" for a single day than to make a commitment for the rest of our lives, so it's a good idea to take that into account in your training guide. Here's what a typical schedule might look like, for an imaginary runner who's working at a stressful job, who is a little overweight, and who hopes to break 41 minutes for 10K in two weeks. He's decided to set as his goals:

1. losing 3 pounds a week (weekly goal) by eliminating alcohol and sugar from his diet (daily subgoals)
2. handling the combination of job stress and training stress by relaxation exercises and getting enough sleep (daily subgoals; no objective means to assess weekly improvement available)
3. getting physically ready for the race by completing the scheduled workout every day (daily subgoal) and totaling 45 miles each week (weekly goal)

For this runner, a typical weekday entry in his training guide might look like this:

MONDAY		
Relaxation?	A.M.	_√_
	P.M.	_no_
Stretch?	A.M.	_√_
No alcohol?		_√_
No sweets?		_√_
In bed by:	10:15	

	SCHEDULED	ACHIEVED
WORKOUT	8 × 440 in 85 seconds, 440R	8 × 440 in 83.6 average, 440R 2 mile warm-up; 2 mile warm-down = 8 M total.

For the last day of the week, it's a good idea to sum up:

SATURDAY		WEEKLY TOTALS
Relaxation?	A.M. no	5 of 7
	P.M. no	3 of 7
Stretch?	A.M. no	6 of 7
No alcohol?	a beer	2 beers
No sweets	√	√(!)
In bed by:	12:15	10:07 ave.

	SCHEDULED	ACHIEVED	WEEK
WORKOUT	Competition 5–15K	5K in 18:32 5 M total	47 M total

One cardinal rule to remember in the construction of your own training guide is this: *Don't* overestimate your abilities when setting either your

Bruce Glikin's structured training has led him to national age-group medals. (Photograph by Katie Klein)

nonathletic or your athletic goals: your chances of succeeding are greatly diminished when you do. To avoid this error, we suggest that you show your training plan to one of your running buddies or some other qualified individual. Ideally, that person will be a runner, but it is more important that he or she have a good understanding of *you* than of training and coaching theory.

Relaxation

Ernest Hemingway defined heroism as "grace under pressure." Heroes are hard to find nowadays, and so are athletes who can achieve total relaxation. However, the techniques you need to improve your ability to relax and avoid tension are fairly easy to master with practice. They will allow any runner to tap into energy stores not otherwise available and thus improve his or her performance.

Techniques for controlling breathing and concentration, and mind-body modifications (such as biofeedback) have been known for centuries, but until recently they were always taught in conjunction with religious or philosophical principles such as transcendental meditation or the martial arts. During the last twenty years, psychologists have systematically studied the physiological aspects of relaxation, and they have also identified what happens to competitive performance when an athlete isn't relaxed. Sports psychologists say that the difference is merely a matter of your state of mind — and that it is not unusual for stress to trigger the anxiety that produces competitive paralysis.

To counteract this condition, sports psychologists say, learn what relaxes you, and then spend 15 minutes a day in a calm, focused state while you practice relaxation techniques. Such a relaxed state can be achieved with audio tapes, meditation, or self-hypnosis, while sitting or lying down. Whatever your chosen method, try to achieve an "inner quietness." And, they counsel, remember that relaxation techniques (just like stretching and massage) can be *learned* and need to be *practiced.*

A RELAXATION EXERCISE — BEFORE TRAINING AND RACING

As I wrote in *The Self-Coached Runner II*, I was troubled with precompetition anxiety when I was beginning to make a name for myself in

Australian state competition. Fortunately, my coach, Chicks Hensley, was several years ahead of the sports psychologists of the day, and he was able to give me an effective relaxation exercise. I used it successfully through collegiate, national, international, and Olympic competition, and I find it as useful today as I did when Chicks first taught it to me forty years ago. If you don't already have an effective relaxation technique, you might want to try mine as part of your 30-minute warm-up before races and important track workouts:

- Lie down on the ground on your back with your legs slightly apart and your arms stretched out at a 90-degree angle to your body.
- Roll your head to the right and think "Relax" for 5 seconds. Roll your head to the left and think "Relax" for 5 seconds.
- Raise your right forearm, leaving your elbow on the ground, and let your hand droop listlessly at the wrist. Lower your arm to the ground. Repeat with your left arm. Repeat twice more, alternating arms.
- Roll your right foot inward, pointing your toes slightly to the left and keeping your leg relaxed, then roll it to the right. Repeat with the left leg. Repeat twice more, alternating feet.
- Relax your face muscles by smiling. Close your eyes and clear your mind of all thoughts. Relax in this position for thirty seconds.
- Roll over to "all fours" and slowly stand up straight.
- Breathe deeply and quietly three times.
- Repeat entire exercise once more.

LEISURETIME RELAXATION EXERCISES

One advance that has been made in relaxation techniques since Chicks Hensley's day is the realization that a runner's ability to use precompetition relaxation is enhanced by regular use of daily relaxation drills. Daily relaxation drills have the added benefit of allowing runners to let go of the physical and emotional stress caused by normal daily activities.

The following technique is one recommended by sports psychologist Kirk Coverstone, whose competitive career is discussed earlier in this chapter. The techniques he recommends, and the principles underlying them, are widely used by sports psychologists across the nation. If you already have such a relaxation program, continue to use it. If you do not, you may find the following exercise helpful in overcoming the stress and tension produced in everyday life and in augmenting the relaxation techniques you use just before competition.

- First, find a comfortable position, either sitting or lying down. Make sure your head is supported and your head, neck, and back are in a straight line. Your legs should not be crossed. Your feet should be either supported or placed flat on the floor.
- Close your eyes. Take a deep breath and hold it for the silent count of five. Breathe out. Imagine yourself sinking down, becoming heavier. Take a second breath and hold it for the silent count of eight. Imagine yourself sinking down even further. Think, "Down, down, down." Now take a third breath and hold it for the count of ten. As you breathe out, feel your body relaxing, letting go.
- Focus your attention on the muscles of your eyes. Feel them relaxing and stretching. Imagine them bathed in healing energy (the image frequently suggested by sports psychologists is "pure white light"). As you breathe in, see (in your mind's eye) the energy cascading over your temples, across the top of your scalp, and down the back of your head. As you exhale, feel the warm, relaxing energy leaving behind a pleasant, restful heaviness.
- Now feel the relaxing energy continue its cycle through your neck, through your vocal cords, and down into your chest. It continues through your shoulders and into your upper arms, elbows, forearms, and hands, finally flowing to the tips of your fingers.
- Take another deep breath and hold it for the count of twelve. Breathe out, and sink further into a state of peaceful relaxation. Feel the relaxing energy move down through your chest, lungs, heart, stomach, and down your back. The feeling continues down your spinal cord, into your lower torso, hips, thighs, knees, calves, shins, and finally down through your heels, feet, and toes.
- Take another breath and hold it for a count of fifteen. Repeat the relaxation exercise from the beginning. When you have completed the second cycle, relax for as long as you wish. When you open your eyes, concentrate on being completely relaxed, quiet inside, and at peace physically and mentally.

Visualization

Visualization is a series of mental rehearsals for planned athletic competition (or other important activity) while in a state of conscious dreaming

Leland Dykes practices visualizing smoothness and efficiency. (Photograph by Bruce Glikin)

or controlled imagination. In athletics, the purpose of visualization is to establish an intent or "declaration of purpose."

Sports psychologists and physiologists have established that continuous mental rehearsal creates a memory link between nerve, muscle, and brain, facilitating enhanced biomechanical movement and, hence, enhanced performance. Sometimes called (incorrectly) "muscle memory," this mechanism has proved to be extremely important in training as well as in competition.

I suspect that many runners have already practiced some sort of mental rehearsal; it seems to be a natural human response to an anticipated "big event." But like many athletes of my era, I tried to prevent myself from "running the race over and over in my mind." The coaching philosophy of the fifties was to avoid concentrating intently on competition before the contest, as it was believed that this "fault" led to the depletion of nervous energy needed for the competition. Today we know better.

The following exercise is designed to allow runners to use visualization techniques to establish a calm, relaxed, and focused mental state while "seeing" themselves running their ideal race.

A VISUALIZATION EXERCISE FOR DISTANCE RUNNERS

- See yourself running in an effortless, fluid rhythm. Visualize yourself running lightly over the ground, rather than pounding the surface. As you run you have the feeling of boundless energy, and you feel little discomfort as the miles slip by.
- Next, bring the course you are running into focus. Visualize the terrain and see the spectators. See the colors; smell the smells. Hear the sounds around your body and feel the rhythm of your breathing. Tune in to the sensations of your body and your spirit as you run. See yourself on the course at various points, maintaining your effortless and graceful running style.
- Next, practice deep, smooth breathing while you check your running form. Try to feel your body actually running.
- Finally, run your ideal race over and over in your mind, imagining your feelings of triumph and satisfaction, and the congratulations of those who support your running, after you have successfully completed your race.

WORDS OF CAUTION

In the visualization exercise described above, the key ingredient is "movement." Remember that it is *continuous movement* that establishes the biofeedback connection between nerves, muscles, and the brain. Static visualization ("freezing" the movement) has the effect of paralyzing the biofeedback mechanism, even if the captured movement is biomechanically correct.

Second, visualization affects your training whether you deliberately use it or not. Even the way you feel about a workout can alter its effect on you. If you dread a workout (and hate the coach) and barely manage to drag yourself through it, you *will* get the same cardiovascular benefits and so forth, but you will not benefit from a positive biomechanical feedback response. Put in lay terms, your "muscle memory" of running hard and fast will still be reinforced, but as an unpleasant experience. On the other hand, if you are "psyched up" for a workout and look forward to meeting its challenge, you benefit in two ways: not only will it seem easier to complete, but you will earn the extra benefits of powerful central nervous system reinforcement. It is for this reason that very good coaches like Joe Vigil (Director of Coaching Education for The Athletics Congress of the United States) make a point of talking to their runners before each workout, so that the runners can know *why* they're running any given set of intervals, instead of merely being told to run a certain workout and not ask any questions.

Finally, remember that the technique of visualization shouldn't be used *during* competition. Don't imagine yourself running the final lap when you're on the first one, for example, or you may lose mental contact with the race. And during a race don't concentrate on your running form in order to monitor it; too much performance interpretation can lead to "paralysis by analysis." You've trained for the race, so just race it.

Self-Talk

One of the most important aspects of preparing yourself for competition is becoming aware of your subconscious attitudes toward training and racing. To do that, there are several questions you might ask yourself:

- What is the "voice in your head" saying to you about your running?
- Do you deserve to be successful?
- What do you say to yourself when things go well? When they go poorly?

- Who gets the credit (or blame) for your success (or failure)?
- When you remember a particularly negative experience in your running career, what were you saying about yourself to yourself?
- What recurrent negative beliefs continue to obstruct your running career?

Your answers to these questions are important because (like visualization) your attitudes about yourself (which many sports psychologists call "self-talk") are at work, whether you make use of them or not. Accordingly, you may have a number of negative feelings about your abilities. If you do, the questions above are designed to identify them as the first step in overcoming them.

THINKING THE WORST

In many of us, competition brings out the self-defeating practice of "thinking the worst," and then, in a self-fulfilling prophecy, our worst fears are realized. Even though we might tell ourselves to avoid negative thoughts, we spend too much time thinking "what if . . ." Such thinking usually guarantees the outcome we dread. However, we can change negative thinking into positive thinking and make it work to our advantage.

HOW SELF-TALK CAN WORK FOR YOU

Frances Baxter, M.S.W., a former national-class masters runner, counsels many runners with stress-related problems. She has her clients use the following system to turn self-talk into a productive technique that helps them achieve their goals:

- Tell yourself the positive results you desire for your race.
- Reinforce those goals by telling yourself you deserve them because you've worked hard for them, and that you expect to achieve them.
- Write down your goals, making sure that you make each statement completely positive — that is, rather than saying, "I will finish my marathon without stopping or walking" (using the negative words "stopping" and "walking"), write "I intend to run the entire 26.2 miles."

Frances Baxter.

- If you catch yourself making negative, self-defeating statements, interrupt the thought immediately. Then Baxter recommends that you pretend you are a tape recorder and immediately rewind the tape. Then re-record the statement or thought in a positive form.

SOME DO'S AND DON'TS

- Don't worry if you think *some* negative thoughts. Some worrying is natural.
- Don't punish yourself when negative thoughts creep into your mental preparation. (That will only add to the negativity.)
- Do take time to dwell on the positive side of your competitive preparation.
- Do take the time to write positive statements or affirmations on small cards and place them on prominent places such as dresser mirrors, refrigerators, and bulletin boards to remind yourself of your positive intentions.
- Don't create "all or nothing" goals for yourself, especially those that you may fail to hit early in a race. (For example, if you say, "I'll run under 7 minutes a mile for the entire marathon," and then get a hot, humid day, you may be seriously off pace by six miles. If you put all your eggs in one basket, your marathon could be an omelet before you hit 10K.)
- Do set up a range of goals that takes into account variations in conditions from "great" to "lousy" and variations in your performance from outstanding to acceptable (see pages 57–58).
- Do divide your race into segments and establish reasonable and attainable subgoals for each segment.
- Do remember that, no matter whether or not you manage to accomplish all your goals, it is important to accomplish as many as you can.

Stress and Sports Psychology

In *The Self-Coached Runner II,* we discussed runners who could meet all the qualifying standards necessary to run a mile in less than four minutes but who were unsuccessful in reaching that goal. We had little trouble in explaining why this phenomenon occurs in young athletes: lack of physical maturity and cardiovascular development. The solution to the problem was equally straightforward, as we discussed in the specific case of Leonard Hilton: allow the athlete a few more years to mature while keeping his training consistent and his confidence intact.

During the last decade, I have observed a number of incidents in which *masters* runners were unable to compete at the levels indicated by their qualifying standards. My curiosity aroused, I checked the performances of all my runners, from teenagers to 60-year-olds. I found that a substantially higher percentage of my masters runners were falling below their expected racing performances, even though they had achieved the time standards indicating their readiness to train for given race goals.

Reluctant to accept this situation as a "natural consequence of the aging process," I began to analyze carefully the masters with whom I worked. As I accumulated data, certain small differences began to emerge between masters runners who were successful in achieving their competitive goals and those who fell short. These differences seemed relatively slight and insignificant at first and were sometimes hard to detect, but as I gained more information it became clear that a number of small negative factors can add up to a *large* difference between runners who seem otherwise similar.

A SOLUTION

Soon I was able to construct a model of a runner who — because of many factors, some beyond his control — was significantly handicapped in his quest for realistic time goals in competition. Having identified a number of ingredients that collectively were performance-inhibiting, I was able to design (with the invaluable cooperation of over two hundred athletes) a stress questionnaire for masters runners.

I hope that the following Runners' Stress Questionnaire will become another analytical and practical tool for self-coached runners, enabling them to identify, then eliminate or neutralize, stress factors that affect performance.

As you answer the following questions, remember that the lower the number you achieve, the higher the level of stress in your life. The maximum score on the stress questionnaire is 100, which means "no stress at all." No runner can reasonably expect to achieve that score, unless she has achieved a perfect fusion of her athletics, personal life, and career.

- If you score between 90 and 100, you may attempt any of the schedules (5K, 10K, marathon) in this book without major modification (provided, of course, that you can run the qualifying times indicated at the beginning of each schedule).
- A score of 80 to 89 indicates that some modification is needed in your training. You also need to be aware that your personal stress is approaching a level at which it will harm your racing.
- A score under 80 indicates that the following modifications should be made in any schedule that you qualify to use in your training:

1. Run the time indicated in the schedule *plus the cushion* (see the introduction to the schedules for an explanation of the "cushion"). Thus if your schedule calls for 12 × 440 in :90, run 12 × 440 in :94 (90 seconds plus 4-second cushion = :94).
2. Run the "slow" end of the "easy running" time range. If your schedule calls for "6 easy miles running (7:30 to 8:00 per mile)," run 8:00 per mile.

Training and Racing Stress Questionnaire for Masters Runners

1. What is your body type?
   A. Ectomorph (small bones, stringy, slow-twitch muscles) (Score: 4)
   B. Mesomorph (big bones, heavy, dense, fast-twitch muscle, speed and strength) (Score: 2)
   C. Endomorph (heavy, thick bones and large fat deposits) (Score: 1)   _____
2. How easy was it for you to reach the time standards set out for the schedule you're going to attempt?
   A. Fairly easy (Score: 4)
   B. A struggle (Score: 3)   _____
3. Have you had previous experience in college or high school?
   A. Yes (Score: 2)
   B. No (Score: 1)   _____

4. How is your running weight?
   A. Not overweight (Score: 4)
   B. 1–3 percent overweight (Score: 3)
   C. 4–6 percent overweight (Score: 2)
   D. More than 6 percent overweight (Score: 1)   _____

5. How good is your diet? (See chapter 3.)
   A. Good (Score: 4)
   B. Average (Score: 2)
   C. Poor (Score: 1)   _____

6. Are you predisposed to injury (unable to train for 5 days or more, 3 times in the last year)?
   A. No (Score: 3)
   B. Yes (Score: 1)   _____

7. Do you stretch before and after competition and training?
   A. All the time (Score: 3)
   B. Mostly (75 percent of the time) (Score: 2)
   C. Rarely (Score: 1)   _____

8. Do you warm up and warm down before and after training and competition?
   A. All the time (Score: 3)
   B. Usually (Score: 2)
   C. Rarely (Score: 1)   _____

9. Do you do supplemental exercises (weights, swimming, bicycling)?
   A. Yes (Score: 3)
   B. Occasionally (Score: 2)
   C. Rarely (Score: 1)   _____

10. Ask a qualified person to evaluate your running form. (Is your technique efficient, smooth, and relaxed?)
    A. My form is considered good. (Score: 3)
    B. My form is considered average. (Score: 2)
    C. My form is considered poor. (Score: 1)   _____

11. Do you do physical work in your job? Do you have to travel?
    A. No (Score: 3)
    B. Occasionally (Score: 2)
    C. Yes (Score: 1)   _____

12. Are you a smoker or a former smoker?
    A. Nonsmoker (Score: 5)
    B. Former smoker (Score: 3)
    C. Smoker (Score: 1) _____
13. Are you exposed to allergens, industrial or natural environmental pollutants, or secondhand smoke in your workplace?
    A. No (Score: 4)
    B. Occasionally (Score: 2)
    C. Yes (Score: 1) _____
14. Are your running goals realistic?
    A. Yes (Score: 5)
    B. No (Score: 2) _____
15. Are you running for cosmetic reasons (to lose weight, to look better) or for competitive reasons?
    A. Competitive reasons (Score: 5)
    B. Cosmetic reasons (Score: 2) _____
16. Do you have spouse/partner/family support for your running?
    A. Yes (Score: 5)
    B. Partially (Score: 3)
    C. No (Score: 2) _____
17. Does your job or your profession support or interfere with your running?
    A. Supports (Score: 4)
    B. Neutral (Score: 3)
    C. Interferes (Score: 1) _____
18. Do you feel a lot of mental or physical stress in your job?
    A. No (Score: 3)
    B. Yes (Score: 1) _____
19. Do you have nonfamily support for your running (do your friends run, do you belong to a running club)?
    A. Yes (Score: 5)
    B. No (Score: 3) _____
20. Do you ever feel a compulsion to race excessively?
    A. No (Score: 5)
    B. Yes (Score: 2) _____

21. Do you have a tendency to train harder than your
schedule or your coach recommends?
    A. No (Score: 3)
    B. Yes (Score: 1)   _____
22. Do you recognize and act on symptoms of tiredness and
preinjury soreness?
    A. Yes (Score: 5)
    B. Occasionally (Score: 2)
    C. No (Score: 0)   _____
23. Do you have financial or security worries?
    A. No (Score: 5)
    B. Some (Score: 3)
    C. Yes (Score: 2)   _____
24. When you do not succeed in your competitive or training
goals, do you withdraw, get mad, or act unpleasantly
around friends, family, or clubmates?
    A. No (Score: 5)
    B. Yes (Score: 2)   _____
25. Do you have any sort of chemical dependency (narcotics,
alcohol, prescription drugs)?
    A. No (Score: 5)
    B. Formerly (Score: 3)
    C. Yes (Score: 1)   _____
                              TOTAL SCORE   _____

QUESTIONS AND ANSWERS ABOUT MODIFYING YOUR TRAINING

Q: If I had a low score on the stress questionnaire, should I move down
to the next lower time standard in the race schedules?

A: That might appear to be a logical step, but as a practical matter,
problems of confidence are created when a runner is asked to train
at a lower level than her ability indicates. We strongly recommend
that you continue to use the schedule indicated by your ability —
and modify that schedule according to the "cushion" rule.

Q: Won't the slowing down of my training as I modify my schedule
move that ultimate time goal out of my reach?

A: Not necessarily. The major factors you need to worry about are
(1) the length of time that you spend on the modified schedule, (2)

your ability to handle your personal stress problems, and (3) your inherent cardiovascular development (the more "natural" talent runners possess, the better they seem to be able to overcome non-competitive stress).

THE FUTURE

It should be obvious by this point that sports psychology can improve competitive skills in every segment of American sports, including masters running. But it has other advantages, too. At a recent sports psychology seminar, Kirk Coverstone concluded his talk with these remarks:

> Your running performance is not an index of your worth as a human being. Never forget that running is something you do to mature and test character and enhance the quality of your life — not detract from it.
>
> The only standards we reach, or fail to reach, are our own. You should never lose the ability to enjoy yourself as you push beyond personal, self-limiting beliefs.
>
> Ultimately, the limits we all test are the limits of our ability to endure pain, to battle physical exhaustion, and — equally important — to overcome our mental barriers.

PART II

THE SCHEDULES

CHAPTER 5

Introduction to the Schedules

THE TRAINING SCHEDULES in the next three chapters are divided into three racing distances: 5K, 10K, and marathon.

The schedules for the 5K distance provide specific workouts for athletes attempting to run this distance in the following times: 14:30, 15:30, 16:30, 17:30, 18:30, 19:30, 20:30, 21:30, 22:30, 24:00, 26:00, 28:00, 30:00.

The schedules for the 10K distance provide specific workouts for athletes attempting to run this distance in the following times: 31:00, 33:00, 35:00, 37:00, 39:00, 41:00, 43:00, 46:00, 49:00, 51:30, 54:00, 58:00.

The schedules for the marathon distance provide specific workouts for athletes attempting to run the distance in the following times: 2:25, 2:35, 2:45, 2:55, 3:05, 3:15, 3:25, 3:35, 3:45, 3:55, 4:05, 4:25, 4:50.

The schedules for all distances (5K, 10K, marathon) consist of two parts: an initial 6- to 10-week training base followed by 6 to 10 weeks of specialized training.

Each of the track workouts in the following chapters should be preceded by a warm-up and stretching routine, which prepares the body for the stress of the faster track running. (See pages 23-37 and 82 for a more detailed discussion of the warm-up, warm-down, and stretching.)

In all the schedules, "Day 1" is assumed to be a Sunday.

Using the Schedules

All the schedules (5K, 10K, marathon) listed in these chapters have empirically established shorter-distance time standards that should be met (or have been recently achieved) before the specific training for any of the listed time goals is attempted.

Each individual schedule is preceded by the notation "You are ready to train for _____ if you can run _____," information that will point you to the appropriate training schedule.

THE BEGINNER

Before attempting any of the specific schedules in the following chapters, you should first establish a one-month running base of 75 to 125 miles of easy jogging. Every second training day, you should incorporate 5 to 8 fast and controlled strides of 60 to 100 yards. This base training will initiate the process of strengthening and developing your cardiovascular and musculoskeletal systems. After this initial training period you may attempt the preschedule time standards for the appropriate schedule.

THE EXPERIENCED RUNNER

If you are an experienced runner and you have *previously* attained the recommended qualifying standards for a particular time goal, you can begin the appropriate schedule immediately, providing:

- your training and competitive ability has not substantially deteriorated since you achieved those standards
- too much time has not elapsed since you achieved the standards

THE SCHEDULE "CUSHION"

It is important to remember that all the schedules in the following chapters have a built-in time "cushion." I have established and verified this cushion after many years of personal experimentation as a competitor and coach. The formula is as follows:

For distances up to and including 1 mile, you may exceed or fall short of the scheduled times up to 4 seconds per quarter. Thus each workout in the schedules falls into a range of acceptable times:

- 3 × 1 mile run in 6:00 = 3 × 1 mile in 5:44 to 6:16 (4 seconds × 4 quarters in a mile = a 16-second range)

- 5 × 880 in 2:50 = 5 × 880 in 2:42 to 2:58 (4 seconds × 2 quarters in a half mile [or 880] = an 8-second range)
- 12 × 220 in 39 seconds = 12 × 220 in 37–41 seconds (4 seconds × .5 quarter = a 2-second range)

For distances over 1 mile, you may exceed or fall short of the scheduled times by 2 seconds per quarter:

- 2 × 3 miles in 18:00 = 2 × 3 miles in 17:36 to 18:24 (12 quarters × 2 seconds = a 24-second range)
- 3 × 1.5 miles in 8:30 = 3 × 1.5 miles in 8:18 to 8:42 (6 quarters × 2 seconds = a 12-second range)

TRAINING DISTANCES AND "RECOVERY"

Distances in the track workout schedules are all given in yards. We are aware that most of the newer-constructed tracks are metric, but 100 meters is close to 110 yards, 200 meters is close to 220 yards, and 400 meters is only slightly shorter than 440 yards.

The track workouts in all of the schedules that follow are expressed in the following manner: number of repetitions, distance of the repetition, and the recovery between repetitions. Thus "12 × 220 in :31 — 440 R" instructs the athlete to run 220 yards 12 times in 31 seconds each, with a 440-yard recovery in between each 220 yards. The recovery should always be jogged unless otherwise stated.

Schedule Terminology

Strides — short distances (60 to 130 yards) that you run at a fast and controlled pace. Not an all-out sprint.

Strength Runs — faster-paced runs of several miles, which may be separate or incorporated into longer, slower runs. Thus, a schedule may say: "10 miles incorporating 5 miles in 30:00." This means that at some point in your 10-mile run you will increase your pace to 6 minutes per mile and run 5 miles at that pace without stopping. All other parts of your 10-mile run will consist of easy running.

Controlled-Pace Runs — disciplined, even-pace runs slightly under or slightly over your racing distance up to 30K. The pace-per-mile is 15 to 30 seconds slower than your anticipated race pace.

Easy Running — the per-mile pace of "easy running" varies with the ability of individuals and the attempted schedule, therefore the range of acceptable times is always indicated at the beginning of each schedule.

Time Trial — an effort at a given distance in which you run as fast as you can.

Recovery — the amount of distance you may jog between any training effort (or interval). The recovery should be a comfortable, slow pace that allows you to maintain good running form. (Occasionally, it is acceptable to walk for the first part of the recovery distance after a stressful interval effort.)

The Warm-up and the Warm-down

The warm-up is designed to prepare the runner physiologically and psychologically for track training sessions and racing. The warm-up routine should be kept consistent; however, minor adjustments can be made for prevailing weather conditions: shorten in hot weather, lengthen in cold weather. The distance covered in the warm-up should be half a mile to 2 miles, and the runner should practice every type of expected running in her training and racing: disciplined pacing, accelerating, and sprinting. The duration of the warm-up should be 15 to 30 minutes, include a stretching routine, and be timed to conclude 10 minutes before any race. (A track training session, however, may begin immediately following the warm-up routine.)

All races and track training sessions should be concluded with a warm-down consisting of slow jogging for at least one mile and should include light stretching. The purpose of the warm-down is to promote the process of removing chemical fatigue products from the runner's stressed leg muscles through the circulatory system.

Saving a Workout

Every runner sometimes encounters difficulty in completing a scheduled workout. Masters, in particular, are more likely to experience this phenomenon. Unfortunately, the "failure" to complete a scheduled workout usually creates more of a psychological stress than any physiological loss.

Many years ago I adopted a simple rule to prevent any sort of psychological stress from a lost workout. I find this solution is still effective today.

For example, you have 3 × 1 mile in _____ minutes, with an 880-yard recovery on your schedule. As you begin the workout you begin to struggle to hold the scheduled pace. You have trouble completing the interval in the designated time or you run slower than the target time.

During your recovery, you evaluate the situation and come to the conclusion that you cannot complete the workout as scheduled, but you can "save" or "salvage" your workout. You are unable to run another interval mile, but you might be able to run an 880 at your designated mile pace. After another 880-yard recovery, you might try 2 × 440 with a 440-yard recovery. Then you might try 4 × 220 with a 440-yard recovery, before you end your workout.

Although you have not done the designated workout, you have, nevertheless, completed a satisfactory and respectable training session. You have, in effect, "saved" or "salvaged" your workout.

David Jansen, researcher. (Photograph by Paula Jansen Fine Arts Portraits)

CHAPTER 6

Schedules for 5 Kilometers

The 14-Minute 30-Second 5K

You are ready to train for a 14-minute 30-second 5K if you can run:

440 yards in 57 seconds
1 mile in 4 minutes 20 seconds

To run 5K in 14 minutes 30 seconds you need to average 4:40 per mile.

In the first eight weeks of training for this event, you should establish a base of 55 to 65 miles a week. A typical week's training during this period should include:

- one long stamina run of 9 to 13 miles at 6:30 to 6:45 per mile
- one controlled-pace run of 5 to 8 miles at 5:25 to 5:40 per mile
- two endurance workouts on the track consisting of *one* of the following per workout:

  - 20 × 110 yards in 15 seconds, with a 220-yard recovery in between
  - 12 × 220 yards in 33 seconds, with a 220-yard recovery in between
  - 16 × 440 yards in 78 seconds, with a 220-yard recovery in between

. 8 × 880 yards in 2 minutes 35 seconds, with a 440-yard recovery in between

. 5 × 1 mile in 5 minutes 20 seconds, with a 660-yard recovery in between

. 440 yards in 75 seconds; 880 yards in 2 minutes 35 seconds; ¾ mile in 4 minutes 5 seconds; 1 mile in 5 minutes 25 seconds — all with 440 yards recovery in between; jog 880 yards; 1 mile in 5 minutes 10 seconds; ¾ mile in 3 minutes 45 seconds; 880 yards in 2 minutes 20 seconds; 440 yards in 68 seconds — all with 440 yards recovery in between

• three days of easy running (6 to 9 miles) at 6:30 to 6:45 per mile

Select one short-distance (110 to 440 yards) and one medium-distance (880 yards to 1 mile) endurance workout in each week's training.

During the first eight-week training period, you should attempt 4 races at distances of 2 miles to 15K. These races should replace an "easy running" day.

At this level of running excellence you also have the option of adding two morning runs of 3 to 5 miles each on nontrack days, incorporating 6 to 10 fast and controlled strides of 70 to 100 yards.

FINAL EIGHT-WEEK SCHEDULE

"Easy running" in this schedule is 6:30 to 6:45 per mile.

1st Week

Day

1 12 miles easy running
2 12 × 220 in :31 — 440 R
3 6 miles easy running
4 6 × 880 in 2:25 — 660 R
5 6 miles easy running
6 6 miles incorporating 2 × 1 mile in 5:00
7 10 miles in 60:00

2nd Week

Day

1 8 miles incorporating 8 × 100 (fast and controlled)
2 660 in 1:45 — 110 R; 220 in :32 — 550 R. Repeat set 4 more times
3 8 miles in 48:00
4 10 × 440 in :66 — 440 R
5 8 miles easy running
6 Rest day
7 Competitive effort: 2 miles to 10K

3rd Week

Day

1 10 miles easy running
2 20 × 110 in :16 — 110 R
3 6 miles incorporating 2 × 1 mile in 5:00
4 8 miles easy running

5   6 × 440 in :63 — 440 R
6   6 miles easy running
7   8 miles incorporating 10 × 100 (fast and controlled)

4th Week
Day

1   12 miles easy running
2   5 miles easy running
3   2-mile time trial
4   6 miles easy running
5   6 miles incorporating 8 × 100 (fast and controlled)
6   6 miles easy running
7   4 × 1 mile in 5:00 — 660 R

5th Week
Day

1   10 miles easy running
2   16 × 440 in :70 — 440 R
3   6 miles easy running
4   2 × 1 mile in 4:38 — 1-mile R
5   6 miles easy running
6   Rest day
7   Competitive effort: 2 miles to 10K

6th Week
Day

1   6–10 miles easy running
2   10 × 220 in :30 — 440 R
3   8 miles incorporating 6 miles in 34:00
4   6 miles easy running
5   5 × 880 in 2:18 — 880 R
6   5 miles easy running
7   2 miles in 9:30

7th Week
Day

1   10 miles easy running
2   12 × 110 in :15 — 330 R
3   6 miles easy running
4   3 × 1 mile in 4:50 — 440 R
5   6 miles easy running
6   6 × 440 in :64 — 440 R
7   8 miles easy running

8th Week
Day

1   10 miles in 60:00
2   5 × 880 in 2:18 — 440 R
3   6 miles easy running
4   2 × 1 mile in 4:40 — 1-mile R
5   5 miles easy running
6   Rest day
7   14-minute 30-second 5K

Douglas Appling, physician. (Photograph by Bruce Glikin)

The 15-Minute 30-Second 5K

You are ready to train for a 15-minute 30-second 5K if you can run:

440 yards in 61 seconds
1 mile in 4 minutes 39 seconds

To run a 15-minute 30-second 5K you need to average 4:59 per mile.

In the first eight weeks of training for this event, you should establish a base of 55 to 65 miles a week. A typical week's training during this period should include:

- one long stamina run of 9 to 13 miles at 6:45 to 7:00 per mile
- one controlled-pace run of 5 to 8 miles at 5:40 to 5:55 per mile
- two endurance workouts on the track consisting of *one* of the following per workout:

  - 20 × 110 yards in 16 seconds, with a 220-yard recovery in between
  - 12 × 220 yards in 35 seconds, with a 220-yard recovery in between
  - 16 × 440 yards in 80 seconds, with a 220-yard recovery in between
  - 8 × 880 yards in 2 minutes 38 seconds, with an 880-yard recovery in between
  - 5 × 1 mile in 5 minutes 25 seconds, with an 880-yard recovery in between
  - 2 × 1.5 miles in 8 minutes 15 seconds, with a 1-mile recovery in between

- three days of easy running (6 to 9 miles) at 6:45 to 7:00 per mile
- optional: two morning runs of 3 to 5 miles each on nontrack days, incorporating 6 to 10 fast and controlled strides of 70 to 100 yards

Select one short-distance (110 to 440 yards) and one medium-distance (880 yards to 1.5 miles) endurance workout in each week's training.

During the first eight-week training period, you should attempt 4 races at distances of 2 miles to 15K. These races should replace an easy running day.

FINAL EIGHT-WEEK SCHEDULE

"Easy running" in this schedule is 6:45 to 7:00 per mile.

1st Week

Day

1. 12 miles easy running
2. 12 × 220 in :32 — 440 R
3. 6 miles easy running
4. 6 × 880 in 2:30 — 660 R
5. 6 miles easy running
6. 6 miles incorporating 2 × 1 mile in 5:10
7. 10 miles in 61:30

2nd Week

Day

1. 10 miles easy running
2. 10 × 440 in :70 — 440 R
3. 8 miles in 49:00
4. 8 × 220 in :31 — 440 R
5. 8 miles easy running
6. Rest day
7. Competitive effort: 2 miles to 10K

3rd Week

Day

1. 8 miles easy running
2. 20 × 110 in :16.5 — 110 R
3. 6 miles incorporating 2 × 1 mile in 5:10
4. 6 miles easy running
5. 6 × 440 in :65 — 440 R
6. 6 miles easy running
7. 8 miles easy running

4th Week

Day

1. 12 miles easy running
2. 5 miles easy running
3. 2-mile time trial
4. 6 miles easy running
5. 6 miles incorporating 8 × 100 (fast and controlled)
6. 3 miles easy running
7. 4 × 1 mile in 5:10 — 660 R

5th Week

Day

1. 10 miles easy running
2. 16 × 440 in :74 — 440 R
3. 6 miles easy running
4. 2 × 1 mile in 4:48 — 1-mile R
5. 5 miles easy running
6. Rest day
7. Competitive effort: 2 miles to 10K

6th Week

Day

1. 6–10 miles easy running
2. 8 × 330 in :52 — 220 R
3. 8 miles incorporating 6 miles in 35:00
4. 6 miles easy running
5. 5 × 880 in 2:24 — 880 R
6. 5 miles easy running
7. 2 miles in 10:00

7th Week

Day

1 10 miles easy running
2 10 × 110 in :15.5 — 330 R
3 6 miles easy running
4 3 × 1 mile in 4:58 — 440 R
5 6 miles easy running
6 5 × 440 in :66 — 440 R
7 8 miles easy running

8th Week

Day

1 10 miles in 61:00
2 4 × 880 in 2:24 — 440 R
3 5 miles easy running
4 10 × 220 in :34 — 220 R
5 3 miles easy running
6 Rest day
7 15-minute 30-second 5K

Robert Cozens, producer. (Photograph by Patsy Cravens)

The 16-Minute 30-Second 5K

> *You are ready to train for a 16-minute 30-second 5K if you can run:*
>
> *440 yards in 65.5 seconds*
> *1 mile in 4 minutes 58 seconds*
>
> *To run a 16-minute 30-second 5K you need to average 5:18 per mile.*

In the first eight weeks of training for this event, you should establish a base of 50 to 60 miles a week. A typical week's training during this period should include:

- one long stamina run of 9 to 12 miles at 7:00 to 7:15 per mile
- one controlled-pace run of 4 to 7 miles at 5:55 to 6:10 per mile
- two endurance workouts on the track consisting of *one* of the following per workout:

  - 20 × 110 yards in 17 seconds, with a 220-yard recovery in between
  - 12 × 220 yards in 36 seconds, with a 220-yard recovery in between
  - 16 × 440 yards in 82 seconds, with a 220-yard recovery in between
  - 4 × 1 mile in 5 minutes 35 seconds, with an 880-yard recovery in between
  - 2 × 1.5 miles in 8 minutes 30 seconds, with a 1-mile recovery in between

- three days of easy running (5 to 8 miles) at 7:00 to 7:15 per mile
- optional: two morning runs of 3 to 5 miles each on nontrack days, incorporating 6 to 10 fast and controlled strides of 70 to 100 yards

Select one short-distance (110 to 440 yards) and one medium-distance (880 yards to 1.5 miles) endurance workout in each week's training.

During the first eight-week training period, you should attempt 4 races at distances of 2 miles to 15K. These races should replace an "easy running" day.

FINAL EIGHT-WEEK SCHEDULE

"Easy running" in this schedule is 7:00 to 7:15 per mile.

1st Week

Day

1   12 miles easy running
2   12 × 220 in :34 — 440 R
3   6 miles easy running
4   5 × 880 in 2:35 — 660 R
5   5 miles easy running
6   5 miles incorporating 2 × 1 mile in 5:20
7   10 miles in 62:30

2nd Week

Day

1   8 miles easy running
2   10 × 440 in :73 — 440 R
3   8 miles in 50:00
4   8 × 220 in :33 — 440 R
5   6 miles easy running
6   Rest day
7   Competitive effort: 2 miles to 10K

3rd Week

Day

1   6 miles easy running
2   20 × 110 in :17.5 — 110 R
3   6 miles incorporating 2 × 1 mile in 5:20
4   5 miles easy running
5   6 × 440 in :69 — 440 R
6   5 miles easy running
7   7 miles easy running

4th Week

Day

1   10 miles easy running
2   5 miles easy running
3   2-mile time trial
4   5 miles easy running
5   5 miles incorporating 8 × 100 (fast and controlled)
6   3 miles easy running
7   4 × 1 mile in 5:20 — 880 R

5th Week

Day

1   7 miles easy running
2   12 × 440 in :76 — 440 R
3   6 miles easy running
4   2 × 1 mile in 5:12 — 1-mile R
5   5 miles easy running
6   Rest day
7   Competitive effort: 2 miles to 10K

6th Week

Day

1   5–9 miles easy running
2   8 × 330 in :55 — 440 R
3   8 miles incorporating 6 miles in 35:30
4   5 miles easy running
5   5 × 880 in 2:30 — 880 R
6   5 miles easy running
7   2 miles in 10:50

7th Week

Day

1   10 miles easy running
2   10 × 110 in :16 — 330 R
3   6 miles easy running
4   3 × 1 mile in 5:30 — 440 R
5   6 miles easy running
6   5 × 440 in :68 — 440 R
7   6 miles easy running

8th Week

Day

1   8 miles in 50:00
2   4 × 880 in 2:30 — 660 R
3   6 miles easy running
4   8 × 220 in :35 — 440 R
5   3 miles easy running
6   Rest day
7   16-minute 30-second 5K

Georgette Greene, special-education teacher. (Photograph by Bruce Glikin)

The 17-Minute 30-Second 5K

> *You are ready to train for a 17-minute 30-second 5K if you can run:*
>
> *440 yards in 68 seconds*
> *1 mile in 5 minutes 12 seconds*
>
> *To run a 17-minute 30-second 5K you need to average 5:36 per mile.*

In the first eight weeks of training for this event, you should establish a base of 50 to 60 miles a week. A typical week's training during this period should include:

- one long stamina run of 9 to 12 miles at 7:10 to 7:25 per mile
- one controlled-pace run of 4 to 7 miles at 6:05 to 6:15 per mile
- two endurance workouts on the track consisting of *one* of the following per workout:

  - 20 × 110 yards in 18 seconds, with a 220-yard recovery in between
  - 12 × 220 yards in 38 seconds, with a 220-yard recovery in between
  - 16 × 440 yards in 85 seconds, with a 220-yard recovery in between
  - 6 × 880 yards in 2 minutes 50 seconds, with a 440-yard recovery in between
  - 4 × 1 mile in 5 minutes 50 seconds, with an 880-yard recovery in between

- three days of easy running (5 to 8 miles) at 7:10 to 7:25 per mile
- optional: two morning runs of 3 to 5 miles each on nontrack days, incorporating 6 to 10 fast and controlled strides of 70 to 100 yards

Select one short-distance (110 to 440 yards) and one medium-distance (880 yards to 1 mile) endurance workout in each week's training.

During the first eight-week training period, you should attempt 3 races at distances of 2 miles to 15K. These races should replace an "easy running" day.

FINAL EIGHT-WEEK SCHEDULE

"Easy running" in this schedule is 7:10 to 7:25 per mile.

1st Week

Day

1 12 miles easy running
2 12 × 220 in :36 — 440 R
3 6 miles easy running
4 5 × 880 in 2:40 — 660 R
5 5 miles easy running
6 5 miles incorporating 2 × 1 mile in 5:35
7 10 miles in 64:00

2nd Week

Day

1 7 miles easy running
2 10 × 440 in :75 — 440 R
3 8 miles in 52:00
4 8 × 220 in :34 — 440 R
5 5 miles easy running
6 Rest day
7 Competitive effort: 2 miles to 10K

3rd Week

Day

1 6 miles easy running
2 20 × 110 in :18 — 110 R
3 6 miles incorporating 2 × 1 mile in 5:40
4 5 miles easy running
5 6 × 440 in :73 — 440 R
6 5 miles easy running
7 6 miles easy running

4th Week

Day

1 10 miles easy running
2 5 miles easy running
3 2-mile time trial
4 5 miles easy running
5 5 miles easy running
6 3 miles easy running
7 4 × 1 mile in 5:35 — 880 R

5th Week

Day

1 6 miles easy running
2 12 × 440 in :78 — 440 R
3 6 miles easy running
4 2 × 1 mile in 5:25 — 1-mile R
5 5 miles easy running
6 Rest day
7 Competitive effort: 2 miles to 10K

6th Week

Day

1 5–9 miles easy running
2 8 × 220 in :35 — 440 R
3 8 miles incorporating 6 miles in 36:30
4 3 miles easy running
5 5 × 880 in 2:42 — 880 R
6 5 miles easy running
7 2 miles in 11:30

7th Week

Day

1 8 miles easy running
2 10 × 110 in :16.5 — 330 R
3 6 miles easy running
4 3 × 1 mile in 5:40 — 440 R
5 5 miles easy running
6 5 × 440 in :70 — 440 R
7 6 miles easy running

8th Week

Day

1 8 miles incorporating 2 miles in 11:45
2 3 × 880 in 2:40 — 660 R
3 6 miles easy running
4 6 × 220 in :36 — 440 R
5 3 miles easy running
6 Rest day
7 17-minute 30-second 5K

Joan Walker, health and physical-education teacher. (Photograph by Bruce Glikin)

The 18-Minute 30-Second 5K

You are ready to train for an 18-minute 30-second 5K if you can run:

440 yards in 70 seconds
1 mile in 5 minutes 26 seconds

To run a 5K in 18 minutes 30 seconds you need to average 5:57 per mile.

In the first eight weeks of training for this event, you should establish a base of 45 to 55 miles a week. A typical week's training during this period should include:

- one long stamina run of 9 to 12 miles at 7:25 to 7:40 per mile
- one controlled-pace run of 4 to 7 miles at 6:20 to 6:30 per mile
- two endurance workouts on the track consisting of *one* of the following per workout:

  - 16 × 110 yards in 19 seconds, with a 220-yard recovery in between
  - 12 × 220 yards in 39 seconds, with a 220-yard recovery in between
  - 12 × 440 yards in 86 seconds, with a 440-yard recovery in between
  - 6 × 880 yards in 3 minutes, with a 440-yard recovery in between
  - 3 × 1 mile in 6 minutes 5 seconds, with a 440-yard recovery in between

- three days of easy running (5 to 7 miles) at 7:25 to 7:40 per mile
- optional: two morning runs of 3 to 5 miles each on nontrack days, incorporating 6 to 10 fast and controlled strides of 70 to 100 yards

Select one short-distance (110 to 440 yards) and one medium-distance (880 yards to 1 mile) endurance workout in each week's training.

During the first eight-week period of training, you should attempt 3 races at distances of 2 miles to 15K. These races should replace an "easy running" day.

FINAL EIGHT-WEEK SCHEDULE

"Easy running" in this schedule is 7:25 to 7:40 per mile.

1st Week

Day

1. 10 miles easy running
2. 12 × 220 in :38 — 440 R
3. 5 miles easy running
4. 5 × 880 in 2:45 — 880 R
5. 5 miles easy running
6. 3 miles easy running
7. Competitive effort: 2 miles to 10K

2nd Week

Day

1. 6–9 miles easy running
2. 10 × 330 in :60 — 440 R
3. 7 miles in 47:15
4. 5 × 440 in :78 — 220 R
5. 6 miles easy running
6. Rest day
7. 10 miles incorporating 2 × 2 miles in 12:20

3rd Week

Day

1. 6 miles easy running
2. 20 × 110 in :19 — 110 R
3. 6 miles incorporating 2 × 1 mile in 5:45
4. 6 miles easy running
5. 4 miles easy running
6. 3 miles easy running
7. Competitive effort: 2 miles to 10K

4th Week

Day

1. 6 miles easy running
2. 10 miles in 67:30
3. 6 miles easy running
4. 8 × 220 in :36 — 440 R
5. 5 miles easy running
6. Rest day
7. Competitive effort: 2 miles to 8K

5th Week

Day

1. 8 miles incorporating 2 × 1 mile in 5:45
2. 5 miles easy running
3. 3 × 880 in 2:45 — 880 R
4. 6 miles easy running
5. 6 miles incorporating 2 miles in 12:00
6. 5 × 440 in :78 — 440 R
7. 8 miles easy running

6th Week

Day

1. 6 miles incorporating 2 × 1 mile in 5:45
2. 12 × 110 in :19 — 330 R
3. 5 miles easy running
4. 4 × 440 in :75 — 440 R
5. 4 miles easy running
6. Rest day
7. Competitive effort: 2 miles to 8K

7th Week

Day

1 5–8 miles easy running
2 8 × 330 in :60 — 550 R
3 5 miles easy running
4 3 × 880 in 2:45 — 880 R
5 5 miles easy running
6 5 miles easy running
7 8 miles incorporating 2 miles in 12:00

8th Week

Day

1 8 miles easy running
2 5 × 440 in :76 — 440 R
3 5 miles easy running
4 5 × 220 in :38 — 440 R
5 3 miles easy running
6 Rest day
7 18-minute 30-second 5K

Cheryl Davis, newspaper publisher. (Photograph by Dave Rainey; Courtesy Runner Triathlete News)

The 19-Minute 30-Second 5K

You are ready to train for a 19-minute 30-second 5K if you can run:

440 yards in 73.5 seconds
1 mile in 5 minutes 40 seconds

To run 5K in 19 minutes 30 seconds you need to average 6:16 per mile.

In the first eight weeks of training for this event, you should establish a base of 45 to 55 miles a week. A typical week's training during this period should include:

- one long stamina run of 8 to 12 miles at 7:40 to 8:00 per mile
- one controlled-pace run of 4 to 7 miles at 6:50 to 7:15 per mile
- two endurance workouts on the track consisting of *one* of the following per workout:

  - 16 × 110 yards in 20 seconds, with a 220-yard recovery in between
  - 10 × 220 yards in 40 seconds, with a 220-yard recovery in between
  - 10 × 440 yards in 88 seconds, with a 440-yard recovery in between
  - 5 × 880 yards in 3 minutes 10 seconds, with an 880-yard recovery in between
  - 3 × 1 mile in 6 minutes 25 seconds, with an 880-yard recovery in between

- three days of easy running (5 to 7 miles) at 7:40 to 8:00 per mile

Select one short-distance (110 to 440 yards) and one medium-distance (880 yards to 1 mile) endurance workout in each week's training.

During the first eight-week training period, you should attempt 3 races at distances of 2 miles to 15K. These races should replace an "easy running" day.

FINAL SIX-WEEK SCHEDULE

"Easy running" in this schedule is 7:40 to 8:00 per mile.

1st Week

Day

1 10 miles easy running
2 10 × 220 in :39 — 440 R
3 5 miles easy running
4 5 × 880 in 2:50 — 880 R
5 5 miles easy running
6 3 miles easy running
7 Competitive effort: 2 miles to 10K

2nd Week

Day

1 6–9 miles easy running
2 10 × 330 in :63 — 440 R
3 8 miles incorporating 5 miles in 34:00
4 6 miles easy running
5 5 × 440 in :80 — 440 R
6 Rest day
7 10 miles incorporating 2 × 2 miles in 13:00

3rd Week

Day

1 6 miles easy running
2 20 × 110 in :20 — 110 R
3 6 miles incorporating 2 × 1 mile in 6:00
4 6 miles easy running
5 4 miles easy running
6 3 miles easy running
7 Competitive effort: 2 miles to 10K

4th Week

Day

1 6 miles easy running
2 10 miles in 70:00
3 6 miles easy running
4 8 × 220 in :38 — 440 R
5 5 miles easy running
6 Rest day
7 Competitive effort: 2 miles to 8K

5th Week

Day

1 7 miles incorporating 2 × 1 mile in 6:00
2 5 miles easy running
3 3 × 880 in 2:52 — 880 R
4 6 miles easy running
5 6 miles incorporating 2 miles in 13:00
6 6 miles easy running
7 5 × 440 in :80 — 440 R

6th Week

Day

1 8 miles easy running
2 12 × 110 in :19 — 110 R
3 5 miles easy running
4 4 × 440 in :78 — 440 R
5 3 miles easy running
6 Rest day
7 19-minute 30-second 5K

Cynthia Kendrick, patent attorney. (Photograph by Bruce Glikin)

The 20-Minute 30-Second 5K

You are ready to train for a 20-minute 30-second 5K if you can run:

440 yards in 76.5 seconds
1 mile in 6 minutes 5 seconds

To run a 5K in 20 minutes 30 seconds you need to average 6:35 per mile.

In the first eight weeks of training for this event, you should establish a base of 40 to 50 miles a week. A typical week's training during this period should include:

- one long stamina run of 8 to 11 miles at 7:50 to 8:15 per mile
- one controlled-pace run of 4 to 6 miles at 6:55 to 7:15 per mile
- two endurance workouts on the track consisting of *one* of the following per workout:

  - 16 × 110 yards in 21 seconds, with a 220-yard recovery in between
  - 10 × 220 yards in 42 seconds, with a 220-yard recovery in between
  - 8 × 440 yards in 89 seconds, with a 440-yard recovery in between
  - 4 × 880 yards in 3 minutes 15 seconds, with an 880-yard recovery in between
  - 3 × 1 mile in 6 minutes 45 seconds, with an 880-yard recovery in between

- three days of easy running (4 to 6 miles) at 7:50 to 8:15 per mile

Select one short-distance (110 to 440 yards) and one medium-distance (880 yards to 1 mile) endurance workout in each week's training.

During the first eight-week training period, you should attempt 3 races at distances of 2 miles to 15K. These races should replace an "easy running" day.

FINAL SIX-WEEK SCHEDULE

"Easy running" in this schedule is 7:50 to 8:15 per mile.

1st Week

Day

1 10 miles easy running
2 10 × 220 in :40 — 440 R
3 5 miles easy running
4 4 × 880 in 3:06 — 880 R
5 6 miles easy running
6 Rest day
7 Competitive effort: 2 miles to 10K

2nd Week

Day

1 5–8 miles easy running
2 8 × 330 in :64 — 440 R
3 8 miles incorporating 5 miles in 35:00
4 4 × 440 in :82 — 440 R
5 5 miles easy running
6 Rest day
7 10 miles incorporating 2 × 2 miles in 13:30

3rd Week

Day

1 6 miles easy running
2 16 × 110 in :21 — 110 R
3 5 miles easy running
4 5 miles incorporating 2 × 1 mile in 6:20
5 3 miles easy running
6 Rest day
7 Competitive effort: 2 miles to 10K

4th Week

Day

1 3–6 miles easy running
2 10 miles in 71:30
3 5 miles easy running
4 8 × 220 in :40 — 440 R
5 5 miles easy running
6 Rest day
7 Competitive effort: 2 miles to 8K

5th Week

Day

1 6 miles easy running
2 5 × 440 in :85 — 220 R
3 6 miles easy running
4 3 × 880 in 3:00 — ¾-mile R
5 6 miles easy running
6 Rest day
7 6 miles incorporating 2 miles in 13:30

6th Week

Day

1 7 miles easy running
2 10 × 110 in :20 — 220 R
3 5 miles easy running
4 4 × 440 in :82 — 440 R
5 3 miles easy running
6 Rest day
7 20-minute 30-second 5K

Cathy Johns, homemaker. (Photograph by Bruce Glikin)

The 21-Minute 30-Second 5K

You are ready to train for a 21-minute 30-second 5K if you can run:

440 yards in 79.5 seconds
1 mile in 6 minutes 22 seconds

To run 5K in 21 minutes 30 seconds you need to average 6:55 per mile.

In the first six weeks of training for this event, you should establish a base of 40 to 50 miles a week. A typical week's training during this period should include:

- one long stamina run of 8 to 11 miles at 8:00 to 8:20 per mile
- one controlled-pace run of 4 to 6 miles at 7:15 to 7:30 per mile
- two endurance workouts on the track consisting of *one* of the following per workout:

  - 16 × 110 yards in 21 seconds, with a 330-yard recovery in between
  - 10 × 220 yards in 43 seconds, with a 440-yard recovery in between
  - 8 × 440 yards in 90 seconds, with a 440-yard recovery in between
  - 4 × 880 yards in 3 minutes 30 seconds, with an 880-yard recovery in between
  - 3 × 1 mile in 7 minutes 15 seconds, with an 880-yard recovery in between

- three days of easy running (4 to 6 miles) at 8:00 to 8:30 per mile

Select one short-distance (110 to 440 yards) and one medium-distance (880 yards to 1 mile) endurance workout in each week's training.

During the first six-week training period, you should attempt 3 races at distances of 2 miles to 15K. These races should replace an "easy running" day.

FINAL SIX-WEEK SCHEDULE

"Easy running" in this schedule is 8:00 to 8:30 per mile.

1st Week

Day

1 10 miles easy running
2 10 × 220 in :43 — 440 R
3 5 miles easy running
4 4 × 880 in 3:20 — 880 R
5 6 miles easy running
6 Rest day
7 Competitive effort: 2 miles to 10K

2nd Week

Day

1 5–8 miles easy running
2 8 × 330 in :66 — 440 R
3 8 miles incorporating 5 miles in 37:30
4 4 × 440 in :85 — 440 R
5 5 miles easy running
6 Rest day
7 10 miles incorporating 2 × 2 miles in 14:30

3rd Week

Day

1 6 miles easy running
2 12 × 110 in :21 — 110 R
3 5 miles incorporating 2 × 1 mile in 7:10
4 5 miles easy running
5 3 miles easy running
6 Rest day
7 Competitive effort: 2 miles to 8K

4th Week

Day

1 3–6 miles easy running
2 10 miles in 75:00
3 4 miles easy running
4 3 × 880 in 3:15 — 880 R
5 4 miles easy running
6 Rest day
7 Competitive effort: 2 miles to 5 miles

5th Week

Day

1 3–6 miles easy running
2 4 × 440 in :86 — 440 R
3 6 miles easy running
4 3 × 1 mile in 7:00 — 440 R
5 6 miles easy running
6 Rest day
7 6 miles incorporating 2 miles in 14:20

6th Week

Day

1 6 miles easy running
2 10 × 110 in :21 — 220 R
3 5 miles easy running
4 4 × 440 in :85 — 660 R
5 3 miles easy running
6 Rest day
7 21-minute 30-second 5K

Peggy Smith, professor of medicine. (Photograph by Bruce Glikin)

The 22-Minute 30-Second 5K

You are ready to train for a 22-minute 30-second 5K if you can run:

440 yards in 83 seconds
1 mile in 6 minutes 40 seconds

To run a 5K in 22 minutes 30 seconds you need to average 7:13 per mile.

In the first six weeks of training for this event, you should establish a base of 40 to 50 miles a week. A typical week's training during this period should include:

- one long stamina run of 7 to 10 miles at 8:10 to 8:30 per mile
- one controlled-pace run of 4 to 6 miles at 7:40 to 7:55 per mile
- two endurance workouts on the track consisting of *one* of the following per workout:

  - 16 × 110 yards in 22 seconds, with a 330-yard recovery in between
  - 8 × 220 yards in 45 seconds, with a 220-yard recovery in between
  - 8 × 440 yards in 91 seconds, with a 440-yard recovery in between
  - 4 × 880 yards in 3 minutes 40 seconds, with an 880-yard recovery in between
  - 3 × 1 mile in 7 minutes 30 seconds, with an 880-yard recovery in between

- three days of easy running (4 to 6 miles) at 8:10 to 8:30 per mile

Select one short-distance (110 to 440 yards) and one medium-distance (880 yards to 1 mile) endurance workout in each week's training.

During the first six-week training period, you should attempt 2 or 3 races at distances of 2 miles to 15K. These races should replace an "easy running" day.

FINAL SIX-WEEK SCHEDULE

"Easy running" in this schedule is 8:10 to 8:30 per mile.

1st Week

Day

1 10 miles easy running
2 10 × 220 in :44 — 440 R
3 5 miles easy running
4 4 × 880 in 3:30 — 880 R
5 5 miles easy running
6 Rest day
7 Competitive effort: 2 miles to 10K

2nd Week

Day

1 4–6 miles easy running
2 6 × 440 in :88 — 660 R
3 8 miles incorporating 5 miles in 38:30
4 6 × 220 in :43 — 440 R
5 5 miles easy running
6 Rest day
7 8 miles incorporating 2 × 2 miles in 15:00

3rd Week

Day

1 6 miles easy running
2 12 × 110 in :22 — 330 R
3 5 miles incorporating 1 mile in 7:00
4 5 miles easy running
5 3 miles easy running
6 Rest day
7 Competitive effort: 2 miles to 5 miles

4th Week

Day

1 3–6 miles easy running
2 10 miles in 77:30
3 4 miles easy running
4 3 × 880 in 3:30 — 880 R
5 5 miles easy running
6 Rest day
7 Competitive effort: 2 miles to 5 miles

5th Week

Day

1 3–6 miles easy running
2 4 × 440 in :88 — 440 R
3 6 miles easy running
4 3 × 1 mile in 7:10 — 440 R
5 6 miles easy running
6 Rest day
7 6 miles incorporating 2 miles in 14:30

6th Week

Day

1 6 miles easy running
2 10 × 110 in :22 — 220 R
3 5 miles easy running
4 4 × 440 in :88 — 660 R
5 3 miles easy running
6 Rest day
7 22-minute 30-second 5K

Allan Jogerst, petroleum land consultant. (Photograph by Bruce Glikin)

The 24-Minute 5K

In the first six weeks of training for this event, you should establish a base of 35 to 45 miles a week. A typical week's training during this period should include:

- one long stamina run of 7 to 10 miles at 8:45 to 9:15 per mile
- one controlled-pace run of 3 to 5 miles at 8:15 to 8:30 per mile
- two endurance workouts on the track consisting of *one* of the following per workout:

  - 12 × 110 yards in 23 seconds, with a 330-yard recovery in between
  - 8 × 220 yards in 48 seconds, with a 220-yard recovery in between
  - 6 × 440 yards in 96 seconds, with a 440-yard recovery in between
  - 3 × 880 yards in 3 minutes 45 seconds, with an 880-yard recovery in between
  - 2 × 1 mile in 7 minutes 50 seconds, with a 1-mile recovery in between

- three days of easy running (3 to 5 miles) at 8:45 to 9:15 per mile

Select one short-distance (110 to 440 yards) and one medium-distance (880 yards to 1 mile) endurance workout in each week's training.

During the first six-week training period, you should attempt 2 or 3 races of distances of 2 miles to 15K. These races should replace an "easy running" day.

FINAL SIX-WEEK SCHEDULE

"Easy running" in this schedule is 8:45 to 9:15 per mile.

1st Week

Day

1 9 miles easy running
2 6 × 220 in :47 — 440 R
3 5 miles easy running
4 3 × 880 in 3:45 — ¾-mile R
5 4 miles easy running
6 Rest day
7 Competitive effort: 2 miles to 10K

2nd Week

Day

1 3–5 miles easy running
2 6 × 440 in :96 — 440 R
3 6 miles incorporating 4 miles in 32:00
4 5 × 220 in :46 — 440 R
5 4 miles easy running
6 Rest day
7 7 miles incorporating 2 miles in 15:45

3rd Week

Day

1 6 miles easy running
2 10 × 110 in :23 — 330 R
3 5 miles incorporating 1 mile in 7:30
4 4 miles easy running
5 3 miles easy running
6 Rest day
7 Competitive effort: 2 miles to 5K

4th Week

Day

1 3–6 miles easy running
2 8 miles in 65:00
3 3 miles easy running
4 3 × 880 in 3:45 — 880 R
5 4 miles easy running
6 Rest day
7 Competitive effort: 2 miles to 5K

5th Week

Day

1 3–5 miles easy running
2 5 miles easy running
3 4 × 440 in :96 — 440 R
4 5 miles easy running
5 6 miles incorporating 4 miles in 32:00
6 Rest day
7 2 × 1 mile in 7:30 — 1-mile R

6th Week

Day

1 6 miles easy running
2 10 × 110 in :23 — 330 R
3 4 miles easy running
4 4 × 440 in :96 — 440 R
5 3 miles easy running
6 Rest day
7 24-minute 5K

Bobby and Fred Haemisegger, homemaker and investment counselor.
(Photograph by Bruce Glikin)

The 26-Minute 5K

You are ready to train for a 26-minute 5K if you can run:

440 yards in 92 seconds
1 mile in 7 minutes 40 seconds

To run 5K in 26 minutes you need to average 8:22 per mile.

In the first six weeks of training for this event, you should establish a base of 35 to 40 miles a week. A typical week's training during this period should include:

- one long stamina run of 6 to 9 miles at 9:15 to 9:40 per mile
- one controlled-pace run of 3 to 5 miles at 8:45 to 9:00 per mile
- two endurance workouts on the track consisting of *one* of the following per workout:

  - 12 × 110 yards in 24 seconds, with a 330-yard recovery in between
  - 6 × 220 yards in 50 seconds, with a 220-yard recovery in between
  - 5 × 440 yards in 1 minute 42 seconds, with a 440-yard recovery in between
  - 3 × 880 yards in 4 minutes 5 seconds, with an 880-yard recovery in between
  - 2 × 1 mile in 8 minutes 15 seconds, with a 1-mile recovery in between

- three days of easy running (3 to 5 miles) at 9:30 to 10:00 per mile

Select one short-distance (110 to 440 yards) and one medium-distance (880 yards to 1 mile) endurance workout in each week's training.

During the first six-week training period, you should attempt 2 or 3 races at distances of 2 miles to 10K. These races should replace an "easy running" day.

FINAL SIX-WEEK SCHEDULE

"Easy running" in this schedule is 9:30 to 10:00 per mile.

1st Week

Day

1. 8 miles easy running
2. 6 × 220 in :49 — 440 R
3. 5 miles easy running
4. 3 × 880 in 4:00 — 880 R
5. 4 miles easy running
6. Rest day
7. Competitive effort: 2 miles to 10K

2nd Week

Day

1. 3–5 miles easy running
2. 5 × 440 in 1:42 — 440 R
3. 6 miles incorporating 4 miles in 34:30
4. 4 miles easy running
5. 5 × 220 in :48 — 440 R
6. Rest day
7. 6 miles incorporating 2 miles in 17:20

3rd Week

Day

1. 6 miles easy running
2. 10 × 110 in :24 — 110 R
3. 5 miles incorporating 1 mile in 8:00
4. 4 miles easy running
5. 4 miles easy running
6. 5 miles incorporating 8 × 100 (fast and controlled)
7. 7 miles easy running

4th Week

Day

1. 5 miles easy running
2. 7 miles in 63:00
3. 4 miles easy running
4. 3 × 880 in 3:50
5. 4 miles easy running
6. Rest day
7. Competitive effort: 2 miles to 5K

5th Week

Day

1. 3–5 miles easy running
2. 5 miles easy running
3. 4 × 440 in 1:40 — 440 R
4. 5 miles easy running
5. 6 miles incorporating 3 miles in 25:30
6. Rest day
7. 2 × 1 mile in 8:00 — 1-mile R

6th Week

Day

1. 5 miles easy running
2. 8 × 110 in :24 — 330 R
3. 5 miles easy running
4. 4 × 440 in 1:40 — 880 R
5. Rest day
6. Rest day
7. 26-minute 5K

The 28-Minute 5K

In the first six weeks of training for this event, you should establish a base of 30 to 35 miles a week. A typical week's training during this period should include:

- one long stamina run of 5 to 8 miles at 9:45 to 10:00 per mile
- one controlled-pace run of 3 to 5 miles at 9:15 to 9:30 per mile
- two endurance workouts on the track consisting of *one* of the following per workout:

    - 10 × 110 yards in 25 seconds, with a 330-yard recovery in between
    - 6 × 220 yards in 52 seconds, with a 220-yard recovery in between
    - 5 × 440 yards in 1 minute 48 seconds, with a 440-yard recovery in between
    - 3 × 880 yards in 4 minutes 25 seconds, with an 880-yard recovery in between
    - 2 × 1 mile in 8 minutes 45 seconds, with a 1-mile recovery in between

- three days of easy running (3 to 5 miles) at 9:45 to 10:30 per mile

Select one short-distance (110 to 440 yards) and one medium-distance (880 yards to 1 mile) endurance workout in each week's training.

During the first six-week training period, you should attempt 2 or 3 races at distances of 2 miles to 10K. These races should replace an "easy running" day.

FINAL SIX-WEEK SCHEDULE

"Easy running" in this schedule is 9:45 to 10:15 per mile.

1st Week

Day

1 8 miles easy running
2 6 × 220 in :50 — 440 R
3 5 miles easy running
4 2 × 880 in 4:10 — 880 R
5 4 miles easy running
6 Rest day
7 Competitive effort: 2 miles to 10K

2nd Week

Day

1 3–5 miles easy running
2 5 × 440 in 1:48 — 440 R
3 6 miles incorporating 4 miles in 37:00
4 4 miles easy running
5 5 × 220 in :52 — 440 R
6 Rest day
7 6 miles incorporating 2 miles in 18:40

3rd Week

Day

1 5 miles easy running
2 10 × 110 in :25 — 110 R
3 5 miles incorporating 1 mile in 8:40
4 5 miles easy running
5 2 × 880 in 4:10 — 880 R
6 Rest day
7 7 miles easy running

4th Week

Day

1 5 miles easy running
2 6 miles in 58:00
3 4 miles easy running
4 3 × 880 in 4:20 — 880 R
5 4 miles easy running
6 Rest day
7 Competitive effort: 2 miles to 5K

5th Week

Day

1 3–5 miles easy running
2 4 miles easy running
3 4 × 440 in 1:44 — 440 R
4 5 miles easy running
5 6 miles incorporating 3 miles in 28:00
6 Rest day
7 2 × 1 mile in 9:15 — 1-mile R

6th Week

Day

1 5 miles easy running
2 8 × 110 in :25 — 330 R
3 5 miles easy running
4 4 × 440 in 1:45 — 440 R
5 Rest day
6 Rest day
7 28-minute 5K

The 30-Minute 5K

You are ready to train for a 30-minute 5K if you can run:

440 yards in 1 minute 45 seconds
1 mile in 8 minutes 40 seconds

To run 5K in 30 minutes you need to average 9:38 per mile.

In the first six weeks of training for this event, you should establish a base of 30 to 35 miles a week. A typical week's training during this period should include:

- one long stamina run of 5 to 8 miles at 10:15 to 10:45 per mile
- one controlled-pace run of 3 to 5 miles at 10:00 to 10:15 per mile
- two endurance workouts on the track consisting of *one* of the following per workout:

    - 10 × 110 yards in 26 seconds, with a 330-yard recovery in between
    - 6 × 220 yards in 54 seconds, with a 440-yard recovery in between
    - 2 × 880 yards in 4 minutes 25 seconds, with an 880-yard recovery in between
    - 2 × 1 mile in 10 minutes, with a 1-mile recovery in between

- three days of easy running (3 to 5 miles) at 10:30 to 11:00 per mile

Select one short-distance (110 to 440 yards) and one medium-distance (880 yards to 1 mile) endurance workout in each week's training.

During the first six-week training period, you should attempt 2 or 3 races at distances of 2 miles to 10K. These races should replace an "easy running" day.

FINAL SIX-WEEK SCHEDULE

"Easy running" in this schedule is 10:30 to 11:00 per mile.

1st Week

Day

1   6 miles easy running
2   6 × 220 in :53 — 440 R
3   5 miles easy running
4   2 × 880 in 4:35 — 880 R
5   3 miles easy running
6   Rest day
7   Competitive effort: 2 miles to 10K

2nd Week

Day

1   3–5 miles easy running
2   5 × 440 in 1:58 — 440 R
3   5 miles incorporating 3 miles in 30:00
4   5 miles easy running
5   4 × 220 in :53 — 660 R
6   Rest day
7   6 miles incorporating 2 miles in 19:45

3rd Week

Day

1   5 miles easy running
2   8 × 110 in :25 — 330 R
3   5 miles incorporating 1 mile in 9:00
4   5 miles easy running
5   2 × 880 in 4:30 — 880 R
6   Rest day
7   6 miles easy running

4th Week

Day

1   6 miles easy running
2   5 miles in 51:00
3   3 miles easy running
4   3 × 880 in 4:30 — 880 R
5   4 miles easy running
6   Rest day
7   Competitive effort: 2 miles to 5K

5th Week

Day

1   6 miles easy running
2   5 miles easy running
3   4 × 440 in 1:55 — 660 R
4   5 miles easy running
5   5 miles incorporating 3 miles in 30:00
6   Rest day
7   2 × 1 mile in 9:45 — 1-mile R

6th Week

Day

1   5 miles easy running
2   8 × 110 in :25 — 330 R
3   4 × 440 in 1:55 — 440 R
4   4 miles easy running
5   Rest day
6   Rest day
7   30-minute 5K

Bill Weaver, certified public accountant. (Photograph by Bruce Glikin)

CHAPTER 7

Schedules for 10 Kilometers

The 31-Minute 10K

You are ready to train for a 31-minute 10K if you can run:

220 yards in 28.5 seconds
440 yards in 60.5 seconds
1 mile in 4 minutes 22 seconds

To run a 10K in 31 minutes you need to average 5:01 per mile.

In the first eight weeks of training for this event, you should establish a base of 65 to 80 miles a week. A typical week's training during this period should include:

- one long stamina run of 12 to 15 miles at 6:35 to 7:10 per mile
- one controlled-pace run of 5 to 8 miles at 5:20 to 5:35 per mile
- two endurance workouts on the track consisting of *one* of the following per workout:

  . 20 × 110 yards in 16 seconds, with a 330-yard recovery in between
  . 12 × 220 yards in 33 seconds, with a 220-yard recovery in between
  . 10 × 440 yards in 70 seconds, with a 440-yard recovery in between

. 5 × 880 yards in 2 minutes 25 seconds, with a 440-yard recovery in between
. 3 × 1 mile in 5 minutes, with an 880-yard recovery in between

• three days of easy running (8 to 12 miles) at 6:35 to 7:10 per mile

Select one short-distance (110 to 440 yards) and one medium-distance (880 yards to 1 mile) endurance workout in each week's training.

Substitute 3 competitive efforts (5K to 20K) for 3 of the "easy running" days during the first eight-week period of 10K training.

FINAL EIGHT-WEEK SCHEDULE

"Easy running" in this schedule is 6:35 to 7:10 per mile.

1st Week

Day

1 15 miles easy running
2 8 × 440 in :67 — 440 R
3 8 miles easy running
4 2 × 2 miles in 10:00 — 1-mile R
5 10 miles easy running
6 7 miles incorporating 8 × 130 (fast and controlled)
7 10 miles incorporating 6 miles in 33:00

2nd Week

Day

1 15 miles easy running
2 20 × 110 in :16 — 110 R
3 10 miles easy running
4 16 × 440 in :78 — 110 R
5 10 miles easy running
6 Rest day
7 Competitive effort: 5K to 20K

3rd Week

Day

1 9–15 miles easy running
2 16 × 220 in :38 — 110 R
3 12 miles easy running
4 8 miles incorporating 4 miles in 22:00
5 6 miles easy running
6 2 sets of 4 × 330 in :47 — 110 between repetitions and 880 between sets
7 10 miles easy running

4th Week

Day

1 16 miles incorporating 10 miles in 57:30
2 6 × 440 in :64 — 440 R
3 8 miles easy running
4 8 × 880 in 2:40 — 220 R
5 10 miles easy running
6 Rest day
7 Competitive effort: 5K to 15K

5th Week

Day

1 9–16 miles easy running
2 25 × 110 in :18 — 110 R
3 10 miles easy running
4 6 miles easy running
5 3 × 1 mile in 4:45 — 440 R

6 6 miles easy running
7 10 miles easy running

6th Week

Day

1 16 miles incorporating 10 miles in 55:00
2 10 × 330 in :50 — 330 R
3 8 miles easy running
4 1 mile in 4:40; ¾ mile in 3:20; 880 in 2:10 — 880 R
5 6 miles easy running
6 Rest day
7 Competitive effort: 5K to 15K

7th Week

Day

1 9–13 miles easy running
2 12 × 220 in :36 — 110 R

3 8 miles easy running
4 10 miles in 57:30
5 8 miles incorporating 6 × 130 (fast and controlled)
6 8 miles incorporating 3 × 1 mile in 5:00
7 8 miles easy running

8th Week

Day

1 10 miles easy running
2 6 × 440 in :68 — 440 R
3 6 miles incorporating 10 × 100 (fast and controlled)
4 6 miles easy running
5 5 miles easy running
6 Rest day
7 31-minute 10K

James McLatchie, computer systems manager. (Photograph by Conrad J. McCarthy)

The 33-Minute 10K

You are ready to train for a 33-minute 10K if you can run:

220 yards in 29.5 seconds
440 yards in 63 seconds
1 mile in 4 minutes 40 seconds

To run a 10K in 33 minutes you need to average 5:20 per mile.

In the first eight weeks of training for this event, you should establish a base of 65 to 75 miles a week. A typical week's training during this period should include:

- one long stamina run of 12 to 15 miles at 7:00 to 7:35 per mile
- one controlled-pace run of 5 to 8 miles at 5:40 to 5:55 per mile
- two endurance workouts on the track consisting of *one* of the following per workout:

  - 20 × 110 yards in 17 seconds, with a 330-yard recovery in between
  - 12 × 220 yards in 34 seconds, with a 220-yard recovery in between
  - 10 × 440 yards in 72 seconds, with a 440-yard recovery in between
  - 5 × 880 yards in 2 minutes 30 seconds, with an 880-yard recovery in between
  - 3 × 1 mile in 5 minutes 20 seconds, with an 880-yard recovery in between

- three days of easy running (7 to 12 miles) at 7:00 to 7:45 per mile

Select one short-distance (110 to 440 yards) and one medium-distance (880 yards to 1 mile) endurance workout in each week's training.

Substitute 3 competitive efforts (5K to 20K) for 3 of the "easy running" days during the first eight-week period of 10K training.

FINAL EIGHT-WEEK SCHEDULE

"Easy running" in this schedule is 7:00 to 7:45 per mile.

1st Week

Day

1   15 miles easy running
2   8 × 440 in :70 — 440 R
3   8 miles easy running
4   2 × 2 miles in 10:40 — 1-mile R
5   10 miles easy running
6   6 miles incorporating 8 × 100 (fast and controlled)
7   10 miles incorporating 6 miles in 34:30

2nd Week

Day

1   13 miles easy running
2   16 × 220 in :34 — 220 R
3   10 miles easy running
4   5 × ¾ mile in 3:55 — 660 R
5   8 miles easy running
6   Rest day
7   Competitive effort: 5K to 20K

3rd Week

Day

1   8–13 miles easy running
2   8 × 440 in :80 — 220 R
3   10 miles incorporating 2 × 2 miles in 11:30
4   6 miles easy running
5   8 × 220 in :31–32 — 440 R
6   8 miles easy running
7   10 miles incorporating 3 miles in 16:00

4th Week

Day

1   14 miles easy running
2   6 × 440 in :66 — 440 R
3   8 miles easy running
4   8 × 880 in 2:45 — 440 R
5   10 miles easy running
6   Rest day
7   Competitive effort: 5K to 15K

5th Week

Day

1   9–14 miles easy running
2   20 × 110 in :18 — 220 R
3   10 miles easy running
4   6 miles easy running
5   3 × 1 mile in 4:55 — 440 R
6   6 miles easy running
7   9 miles easy running

6th Week

Day

1   15 miles incorporating 10 miles in 57:30
2   8 × 440 in :72 — 440 R
3   6 miles easy running
4   1 mile in 4:40; ¾ mile in 3:33; 880 in 2:20 — 880 R
5   5 miles easy running
6   Rest day
7   Competitive effort: 5K to 15K

7th Week

Day

1 8–12 miles easy running
2 10 × 220 in :36 — 220 R
3 8 miles easy running
4 10 miles in 60:00
5 6 miles incorporating 6 × 130 (fast and controlled)
6 8 miles incorporating 3 × 1 mile in 5:10
7 7 miles easy running

8th Week

Day

1 10 miles easy running
2 6 × 440 in :70 — 440 R
3 5 miles incorporating 8 × 100 (fast and controlled)
4 5 miles easy running
5 5 miles easy running
6 Rest day
7 33-minute 10K

Mark Scheid, university professor. (Photograph by Susan Sternberg, courtesy Human-Powered Sports)

The 35-Minute 10K

You are ready to train for a 35-minute 10K if you can run:

220 *yards in* 30.5 *seconds*
440 *yards in* 65 *seconds*
1 *mile in* 5 *minutes*

To run a 10K in 35 minutes you need to average 5:40 per mile.

In the first eight weeks of training for this event, you should establish a base of 60 to 70 miles a week. A typical week's training during this period should include:

- one long stamina run of 12 to 14 miles at 7:15 to 7:40 per mile
- one controlled-pace run of 5 to 8 miles at 6:00 to 6:20 per mile
- two endurance workouts on the track consisting of *one* of the following per workout:

  - 20 × 110 yards in 18 seconds, with a 330-yard recovery in between
  - 12 × 220 yards in 35 seconds, with a 400-yard recovery in between
  - 10 × 440 yards in 74 seconds, with a 440-yard recovery in between
  - 5 × 880 yards in 2 minutes 35 seconds, with an 880-yard recovery in between
  - 3 × 1 mile in 5 minutes 40 seconds, with an 880-yard recovery in between

- three days of easy running (7 to 11 miles) at 7:15 to 7:50 per mile

Select one short-distance (110 to 440 yards) and one medium-distance (880 yards to 1 mile) endurance workout in each week's training.

Substitute 3 competitive efforts (5K to 20K) for 3 of the "easy running" days during the first eight-week period of 10K training.

FINAL EIGHT-WEEK SCHEDULE

"Easy running" in this schedule is 7:15 to 7:50 per mile.

1st Week

Day

1 14 miles easy running
2 8 × 440 in :73 — 440 R
3 8 miles easy running
4 2 × 2 miles in 11:00 — 1-mile R
5 5 miles incorporating 10 × 100 (fast and controlled)
6 8 miles easy running
7 10 miles incorporating 6 miles in 36:00

2nd Week

Day

1 12 miles easy running
2 12 × 220 in :37 — 220 R
3 10 miles easy running
4 5 × ¾ mile in 4:05 — 660 R
5 6 miles easy running
6 Rest day
7 Competitive effort: 5K to 20K

3rd Week

Day

1 8–12 miles easy running
2 8 × 440 in :82 — 220 R
3 10 miles incorporating 2 × 2 miles in 11:45
4 6 miles easy running
5 8 × 220 in :33 — 440 R
6 6 miles easy running
7 10 miles incorporating 3 miles in 17:00

4th Week

Day

1 13 miles easy running
2 6 × 440 in :69 — 440 R
3 8 miles easy running
4 8 × 880 in 2:50 — 660 R
5 6 miles easy running
6 Rest day
7 Competitive effort: 5K to 10K

5th Week

Day

1 9–13 miles easy running
2 20 × 110 in :19 — 220 R
3 10 miles easy running
4 6 miles easy running
5 3 × 1 mile in 5:25 — 440 R
6 6 miles easy running
7 9 miles easy running

6th Week

Day

1 13 miles incorporating 10 miles in 60:00
2 6 miles easy running
3 8 × 440 in :74 — 440 R
4 6 miles incorporating 8 × 100 (fast and controlled)
5 5 miles easy running
6 Rest day
7 Competitive effort: 5K to 15K

7th Week

Day

1 8–12 miles easy running
2 10 × 220 in :38 — 220 R
3 6 miles easy running
4 10 miles in 62:30
5 6 miles easy running
6 7 miles incorporating 3 × 1 mile in 5:30
7 8 miles easy running

8th Week

Day

1 10 miles easy running
2 6 × 440 in :73 — 440 R
3 6 miles incorporating 6 × 100 (fast and controlled)
4 6 miles easy running
5 3 miles easy running
6 Rest day
7 35-minute 10K

Anna Thomsen, massage therapist. (Photograph by Bruce Glikin)

The 37-Minute 10K

You are ready to train for a 37-minute 10K if you can run:

220 *yards in 31.5 seconds*
440 *yards in 67 seconds*
1 *mile in 5 minutes 20 seconds*

To run 10K in 37 minutes you need to average 5:59 per mile.

In the first eight weeks of training for this event, you should establish a base of 55 to 65 miles a week. A typical week's training during this period should include:

- one long stamina run of 11 to 13 miles at 7:30 to 8:00 per mile
- one controlled-pace run of 5 to 8 miles at 6:20 to 6:35 per mile
- two endurance workouts on the track consisting of *one* of the following per workout:

  - 20 × 110 yards in 19 seconds, with a 330-yard recovery in between
  - 12 × 220 yards in 36 seconds, with a 440-yard recovery in between
  - 10 × 440 yards in 76 seconds, with a 440-yard recovery in between
  - 5 × 880 yards in 2 minutes 40 seconds, with an 880-yard recovery in between
  - 3 × 1 mile in 6 minutes, with an 880-yard recovery in between

- three days of easy running (6 to 10 miles) at 7:30 to 8:00 per mile

Select one short-distance (110 to 440 yards) and one medium-distance (880 yards to 1 mile) endurance workout in each week's training.

Substitute 3 competitive efforts (5K to 20K) for 3 of the "easy running" days during the first eight-week period of 10K training.

FINAL EIGHT-WEEK SCHEDULE

"Easy running" in this schedule is 7:30 to 8:00 per mile.

1st Week

Day

1. 14 miles easy running
2. 8 × 440 in :75 — 440 R
3. 7 miles easy running
4. 2 × 2 miles in 11:30 — 1-mile R
5. 7 miles easy running
6. 5 miles incorporating 8 × 100 (fast and controlled)
7. 10 miles incorporating 6 miles in 38:00

2nd Week

Day

1. 12 miles easy running
2. 12 × 220 in :38 — 220 R
3. 8 miles easy running
4. 4 × ¾ mile in 4:15 — 880 R
5. 4 miles easy running
6. Rest day
7. Competitive effort: 5K to 20K

3rd Week

Day

1. 7–10 miles easy running
2. 8 × 440 in :84 — 220 R
3. 10 miles incorporating 2 × 1 mile in 5:45
4. 5 miles easy running
5. 6 × 220 in :34 — 440 R
6. 6 miles easy running
7. 10 miles incorporating 3 miles in 17:45

4th Week

Day

1. 12 miles easy running
2. 6 × 440 in :72 — 440 R
3. 7 miles easy running
4. 6 × 880 in 3:00 — 660 R
5. 5 miles easy running
6. Rest day
7. Competitive effort: 5K to 15K

5th Week

Day

1. 8–12 miles easy running
2. 20 × 110 in :20 — 220 R
3. 10 miles easy running
4. 5 miles easy running
5. 3 × 1 mile in 5:50 — 440 R
6. 5 miles easy running
7. 6 miles easy running

6th Week

Day

1. 13 miles incorporating 10 miles in 64:00
2. 6 miles easy running
3. 8 × 440 in :78 — 440 R
4. 5 miles incorporating 8 × 100 (fast and controlled)
5. 5 miles easy running
6. Rest day
7. Competitive effort: 5K to 15K

7th Week

Day

1 8–12 miles easy running
2 6 × 330 in :56 — 330 R
3 5 miles easy running
4 10 miles in 65:00
5 5 miles easy running
6 7 miles incorporating 3 × 1 mile in 5:50
7 9 miles easy running

8th Week

Day

1 9 miles easy running
2 6 × 440 in :76 — 440 R
3 6 miles incorporating 6 × 100 (fast and controlled)
4 5 miles easy running
5 4 miles easy running
6 Rest day
7 37-minute 10K

Hersh Levitt, master builder. (Photograph by Bruce Glikin)

The 39-Minute 10K

> *You are ready to train for a 39-minute 10K if you can run:*
>
> 220 *yards in 34 seconds*
> 440 *yards in 72.5 seconds*
> 1 *mile in 5 minutes 42 seconds*
>
> *To run a 10K in 39 minutes you need to average 6:19 per mile.*

In the first eight weeks of training for this event, you should establish a base of 50 to 60 miles a week. A typical week's training during this period should include:

- one long stamina run of 11 to 13 miles at 7:45 to 8:15 per mile
- one controlled-pace run of 5 to 8 miles at 6:50 to 7:10 per mile
- two endurance workouts on the track consisting of *one* of the following per workout:

  - 20 × 110 yards in 20 seconds, with a 330-yard recovery in between
  - 12 × 220 yards in 38 seconds, with a 440-yard recovery in between
  - 10 × 440 yards in 79 seconds, with a 440-yard recovery in between
  - 5 × 880 yards in 2 minutes 50 seconds, with an 880-yard recovery in between
  - 3 × 1 mile in 6 minutes 20 seconds, with an 880-yard recovery in between

- three days of easy running (6 to 9 miles) at 7:45 to 8:30 per mile

Select one short-distance (110 to 440 yards) and one medium-distance (880 yards to 1 mile) endurance workout in each week's training.

Substitute 3 competitive efforts (5K to 20K) for 3 of the "easy running" days during the first eight-week period of 10K training.

FINAL EIGHT-WEEK SCHEDULE

"Easy running" in this schedule is 7:45 to 8:30 per mile.

1st Week

Day

1   13 miles easy running
2   8 × 440 in :78 — 440 R
3   6 miles easy running
4   2 × 2 miles in 12:10 — 1-mile R
5   6 miles easy running
6   5 miles incorporating 1 mile in 5:50
7   9 miles incorporating 5 miles in 33:45

2nd Week

Day

1   10 miles easy running
2   10 × 220 in :39 — 220 R
3   8 miles easy running
4   3 × 1 mile in 6:00 — 440 R
5   5 miles easy running
6   Rest day
7   Competitive effort: 5K to 20K

3rd Week

Day

1   6–9 miles easy running
2   8 × 440 in :86 — 220 R
3   10 miles incorporating 2 × 1 mile in 6:00
4   5 miles easy running
5   6 × 220 in :36 — 440 R
6   Rest day
7   9 miles incorporating 3 miles in 19:30

4th Week

Day

1   12 miles easy running
2   16 × 110 in :20 — 110 R
3   6 miles easy running
4   6 × 880 in 3:10 — 440 R
5   3 miles easy running
6   Rest day
7   Competitive effort: 5K to 15K

5th Week

Day

1   7–10 miles easy running
2   10 × 220 in :40 — 220 R
3   9 miles easy running
4   6 miles easy running
5   3 × 1 mile in 6:00 — 440 R
6   5 miles easy running
7   3 miles easy running

6th Week

Day

1   14 miles incorporating 10 miles in 67:30
2   5 miles easy running
3   8 × 440 in :80 — 440 R
4   6 miles easy running
5   4 miles easy running
6   Rest day
7   Competitive effort: 5K to 15K

7th Week

Day

1 7–11 miles easy running
2 8 × 220 in :40 — 440 R
3 5 miles easy running
4 10 miles in 67:30
5 5 miles easy running
6 7 miles incorporating 3 × 1 mile in 6:10
7 8 miles easy running

8th Week

Day

1 8 miles easy running
2 6 × 440 in :79 — 440 R
3 6 miles incorporating 1 mile in 6:00
4 5 miles easy running
5 4 miles easy running
6 Rest day
7 39-minute 10K

Lloyd Posey, consulting engineer. (Photograph by Bruce Glikin)

The 41-Minute 10K

You are ready to train for a 41-minute 10K if you can run:

220 yards in 35.5 seconds
440 yards in 75 seconds
1 mile in 6 minutes 5 seconds

To run a 41-minute 10K you need to average 6:39 per mile.

In the first eight weeks of training for this event, you should establish a base of 45 to 55 miles a week. A typical week's training during this period should include:

- one long stamina run of 8 to 12 miles at 8:00 to 8:30 per mile
- one controlled-pace run of 5 to 8 miles at 7:20 to 7:40 per mile
- two endurance workouts on the track consisting of *one* of the following per workout:

  . 16 × 110 yards in 20 seconds, with a 330-yard recovery in between
  . 10 × 220 yards in 42 seconds, with a 220-yard recovery in between
  . 8 × 440 yards in 85 seconds, with a 440-yard recovery in between
  . 4 × 880 yards in 3 minutes 5 seconds, with an 880-yard recovery in between
  . 3 × 1 mile in 6 minutes 40 seconds, with an 880-yard recovery in between

- three days of easy running (6 to 8 miles) at 8:00 to 8:30 per mile

Select one short-distance (110 to 440 yards) and one medium-distance (880 yards to 1 mile) endurance workout in each week's training.

Substitute 3 competitive efforts (5K to 20K) for 3 of the "easy running" days during the first eight-week period of 10K training.

FINAL EIGHT-WEEK SCHEDULE

"Easy running" in this schedule is 8:00 to 8:30 per mile.

1st Week

Day

1. 12 miles easy running
2. 8 × 440 in :84 — 440 R
3. 5 miles easy running
4. 2 × 2 miles in 13:00 — 1-mile R
5. 5 miles easy running
6. 5 miles incorporating 1 mile in 6:20
7. 8 miles incorporating 3 miles in 20:00

2nd Week

Day

1. 10 miles easy running
2. 8 × 220 in :42 — 220 R
3. 7 miles easy running
4. 3 × 1 mile in 6:20 — 440 R
5. 5 miles easy running
6. Rest day
7. Competitive effort: 5K to 20K

3rd Week

Day

1. 6–9 miles easy running
2. 8 × 440 in :90 — 220 R
3. 8 miles incorporating 2 × 1 mile in 6:20
4. 5 miles easy running
5. 6 × 220 in :38 — 440 R
6. Rest day
7. 8 miles incorporating 3 miles in 19:45

4th Week

Day

1. 10 miles easy running
2. 16 × 110 in :20 — 110 R
3. 5 miles easy running
4. 5 × 880 in 3:15 — 880 R
5. 3 miles easy running
6. Rest day
7. Competitive effort: 5K to 15K

5th Week

Day

1. 6–9 miles easy running
2. 8 × 220 in :42 — 220 R
3. 8 miles easy running
4. 5 miles easy running
5. 3 × 1 mile in 6:20 — 440 R
6. 4 miles easy running
7. 3 miles easy running

6th Week

Day

1. 13 miles incorporating 10 miles in 70:00
2. 5 miles easy running
3. 8 × 440 in :85 — 440 R
4. 6 miles easy running
5. 3 miles easy running
6. Rest day
7. Competitive effort: 5K to 15K

7th Week

Day

1 6–10 miles easy running
2 8 × 220 in :42 — 440 R
3 4 miles easy running
4 10 miles in 69:00
5 5 miles easy running
6 6 miles incorporating 2 × 1 mile in 6:30
7 7 miles easy running

8th Week

Day

1 8 miles easy running
2 6 × 440 in :84 — 440 R
3 5 miles incorporating 1 mile in 6:20
4 4 miles easy running
5 3 miles easy running
6 Rest day
7 41-minute 10K

Connie Coffelt-Lawrence, graphic artist. (Photograph by Bruce Glikin)

The 43-Minute 10K

You are ready to train for a 43-minute 10K if you can run:

220 yards in 36.5 seconds
440 yards in 80 seconds
1 mile in 6 minutes 22 seconds

To run 10K in 43 minutes you need to average 6:57 per mile.

In the first eight weeks of training for this event, you should establish a base of 40 to 50 miles a week. A typical week's training during this period should include:

- one long stamina run of 8 to 11 miles at 8:15 to 8:45 per mile
- one controlled-pace run of 4 to 8 miles at 7:45 to 8:00 per mile
- two endurance workouts on the track consisting of *one* of the following per workout:

  - 16 × 110 yards in 21 seconds, with a 330-yard recovery in between
  - 10 × 220 yards in 43 seconds, with a 440-yard recovery in between
  - 8 × 440 yards in 87 seconds, with a 440-yard recovery in between
  - 4 × 880 yards in 3 minutes 10 seconds, with an 880-yard recovery in between
  - 3 × 1 mile in 7 minutes, with an 880-yard recovery in between

- three days of easy running (5 to 8 miles) at 8:15 to 8:45 per mile

Select one short-distance (110 to 440 yards) and one medium-distance (880 yards to 1 mile) endurance workout in each week's training.

Substitute 3 competitive efforts (5K to 20K) for 3 of the "easy running" days during the first eight-week period of 10K training.

FINAL EIGHT-WEEK SCHEDULE

"Easy running" in this schedule is 8:15 to 8:45 per mile.

1st Week

Day

1 11 miles easy running
2 8 × 440 in :86 — 440 R
3 5 miles easy running
4 2 × 2 miles in 13:30 — 1-mile R
5 5 miles easy running
6 4 miles incorporating 1 mile in 6:40
7 8 miles incorporating 3 miles in 21:00

2nd Week

Day

1 10 miles easy running
2 8 × 220 in :43 — 220 R
3 6 miles easy running
4 3 × 1 mile in 6:40 — 440 R
5 4 miles easy running
6 Rest day
7 Competitive effort: 5K to 20K

3rd Week

Day

1 5–8 miles easy running
2 6 × 440 in :92 — 220 R
3 7 miles incorporating 2 × 1 mile in 6:35
4 5 miles easy running
5 6 × 220 in :40 — 440 R
6 Rest day
7 7 miles incorporating 3 miles in 20:30

4th Week

Day

1 8 miles easy running
2 16 × 110 in :20 — 110 R
3 5 miles easy running
4 4 × 880 in 3:15 — 880 R
5 3 miles easy running
6 Rest day
7 Competitive effort: 5K to 15K

5th Week

Day

1 6–9 miles easy running
2 8 × 220 in :43 — 220 R
3 7 miles easy running
4 4 miles easy running
5 3 × 1 mile in 6:35 — 440 R
6 4 miles easy running
7 3 miles easy running

6th Week

Day

1 12 miles incorporating 10 miles in 72:30
2 5 miles easy running
3 8 × 440 in :88 — 440 R
4 5 miles easy running
5 4 miles easy running
6 Rest day
7 Competitive effort: 5K to 10K

7th Week

Day

1   5–8 miles easy running
2   6 × 330 in :64 — 330 R
3   4 miles easy running
4   10 miles in 72:30
5   4 miles easy running
6   6 miles incorporating 2 × 1 mile in 6:45
7   7 miles easy running

8th Week

Day

1   6 miles easy running
2   6 × 440 in :85 — 440 R
3   6 miles easy running
4   4 miles easy running
5   3 miles easy running
6   Rest day
7   43-minute 10K

Mary G. Cullen, executive board member, United States Olympic Committee. (Photograph by Bruce Glikin)

The 46-Minute 10K

You are ready to train for a 46-minute 10K if you can run:

220 yards in 38.5 seconds
440 yards in 84 seconds
1 mile in 6 minutes 42 seconds

To run a 10K in 46 minutes you need to average 7:26 per mile.

In the first eight weeks of training for this event, you should establish a base of 40 to 50 miles a week. A typical week's training during this period should include:

- one long stamina run of 8 to 11 miles at 8:40 to 9:00 per mile
- one controlled-pace run of 4 to 8 miles at 8:05 to 8:20 per mile
- two endurance workouts on the track consisting of *one* of the following per workout:

    . 16 × 110 yards in 22 seconds, with a 330-yard recovery in between
    . 10 × 220 yards in 44 seconds, with a 440-yard recovery in between
    . 8 × 440 yards in 92 seconds, with a 440-yard recovery in between
    . 4 × 880 yards in 3 minutes 25 seconds, with an 880-yard recovery in between
    . 3 × 1 mile in 7 minutes 30 seconds, with an 880-yard recovery in between

- three days of easy running (5 to 8 miles) at 9:00 to 9:15 per mile

Select one short-distance (110 to 440 yards) and one medium-distance (880 yards to 1 mile) endurance workout in each week's training.

Substitute 3 competitive efforts (5K to 20K) for 3 of the "easy running" days during the first eight-week period of 10K training.

FINAL EIGHT-WEEK SCHEDULE

"Easy running" in this schedule is 9:00 to 9:15 per mile.

1st Week

Day

1 11 miles easy running
2 8 × 440 in :89 — 440 R
3 5 miles easy running
4 2 × 2 miles in 14:30 — 1-mile R
5 5 miles easy running
6 4 miles incorporating 1 mile in 7:00
7 7 miles incorporating 3 miles in 22:30

2nd Week

Day

1 10 miles easy running
2 8 × 220 in :43 — 220 R
3 6 miles easy running
4 3 × 1 mile in 7:00 — 880 R
5 3 miles easy running
6 Rest day
7 Competitive effort: 5K to 20K

3rd Week

Day

1 5–8 miles easy running
2 6 × 440 in :94 — 220 R
3 6 miles incorporating 2 × 1 mile in 7:00
4 5 miles easy running
5 6 × 220 in :42 — 440 R
6 Rest day
7 6 miles incorporating 3 miles in 22:15

4th Week

Day

1 9 miles easy running
2 12 × 110 in :21 — 220 R
3 5 miles easy running
4 4 × 880 in 3:25 — 880 R
5 3 miles easy running
6 Rest day
7 Competitive effort: 5K to 15K

5th Week

Day

1 5–8 miles easy running
2 8 × 220 in :45 — 220 R
3 7 miles easy running
4 4 miles easy running
5 3 × 1 mile in 7:00 — 440 R
6 4 miles easy running
7 3 miles easy running

6th Week

Day

1 12 miles incorporating 10 miles in 77:30
2 8 × 220 in :48 — 220 R
3 5 miles easy running
4 8 × 440 in :92 — 440 R
5 4 miles easy running
6 Rest day
7 Competitive effort: 5K to 15K

7th Week

Day

1   5–8 miles easy running
2   6 × 330 in :68 — 220 R
3   4 miles easy running
4   10 miles in 77:30
5   5 miles easy running
6   5 miles incorporating 2 × 1 mile in 7:00
7   7 miles easy running

8th Week

Day

1   6 miles easy running
2   6 × 440 in :88 — 440 R
3   6 miles easy running
4   4 miles easy running
5   Rest day
6   Rest day
7   46-minute 10K

Harvard Hill, Jr., managing general partner. (Photograph by Scott M. Hill)

The 49-Minute 10K

You are ready to train for a 49-minute 10K if you can run:

220 yards in 40 seconds
440 yards in 86 seconds
1 mile in 7 minutes 5 seconds

To run a 49-minute 10K you need to average 7:55 per mile.

In the first eight weeks of training for this event, you should establish a base of 35 to 45 miles a week. A typical week's training during this period should include:

- one long stamina run of 8 to 11 miles at 8:50 to 9:20 per mile
- one controlled-pace run of 4 to 8 miles at 8:25 to 8:45 per mile
- two endurance workouts on the track consisting of *one* of the following per workout:

  - 16 × 110 yards in 22.5 seconds, with a 330-yard recovery in between
  - 8 × 220 yards in 45 seconds, with a 440-yard recovery in between
  - 6 × 440 yards in 95 seconds, with a 440-yard recovery in between
  - 4 × 880 yards in 3 minutes 45 seconds, with an 880-yard recovery in between
  - 2 × 1 mile in 7 minutes 40 seconds, with an 880-yard recovery in between

- three days of easy running (5 to 7 miles) at 9:20 to 9:45 per mile

Select one short-distance (110 to 440 yards) and one medium-distance (880 yards to 1 mile) endurance workout in each week's training.

Substitute 3 competitive efforts (5K to 20K) for 3 of the "easy running" days during the first eight-week period of 10K training.

FINAL EIGHT-WEEK SCHEDULE

"Easy running" in this schedule is 9:20 to 9:45 per mile.

1st Week

Day

1   10 miles easy running
2   6 × 440 in :92 — 440 R
3   5 miles easy running
4   2 × 2 miles in 15:45 — 1-mile R
5   4 miles easy running
6   4 miles incorporating 1 mile in 7:25
7   6 miles incorporating 3 miles in 23:45

2nd Week

Day

1   8 miles easy running
2   8 × 220 in :45 — 220 R
3   5 miles easy running
4   3 × 1 mile in 7:30 — 880 R
5   3 miles easy running
6   Rest day
7   Competitive effort: 5K to 20K

3rd Week

Day

1   4–7 miles easy running
2   6 × 440 in :97 — 440 R
3   6 miles incorporating 2 × 1 mile in 7:30
4   4 miles easy running
5   6 × 220 in :43 — 440 R
6   Rest day
7   6 miles incorporating 3 miles in 23:45

4th Week

Day

1   9 miles easy running
2   10 × 110 in :22 — 220 R
3   5 miles easy running
4   3 × 880 in 3:40 — 880 R
5   3 miles easy running
6   Rest day
7   Competitive effort: 5K to 15K

5th Week

Day

1   4–7 miles easy running
2   6 × 220 in :46 — 440 R
3   6 miles easy running
4   4 miles easy running
5   3 × 1 mile in 7:25 — 880 R
6   4 miles easy running
7   3 miles easy running

6th Week

Day

1   12 miles incorporating 10 miles in 82:30
2   4 miles easy running
3   8 × 440 in :94 — 440 R
4   5 miles easy running
5   4 miles easy running
6   Rest day
7   Competitive effort: 5K to 15K

7th Week

Day

1 4–7 miles easy running
2 5 × 440 in :98 — 440 R
3 4 miles easy running
4 10 miles in 82:30
5 5 miles easy running
6 Rest day
7 6 miles incorporating 2 × 1 mile in 7:45

8th Week

Day

1 6 miles easy running
2 8 × 220 in :45 — 220 R
3 5 miles easy running
4 5 miles easy running
5 Rest day
6 Rest day
7 49-minute 10K

Karen Thibodeaux, bookkeeper. (Photograph by Bruce Glikin)

The 51-Minute 30-Second 10K

You are ready to train for a 51-minute 30-second 10K if you can run:

220 yards in 41 seconds
440 yards in 88 seconds
1 mile in 7 minutes 30 seconds

To run 10K in 51 minutes 30 seconds you need to
average 8:20 per mile.

In the first eight weeks of training for this event, you should establish a base of 35 to 45 miles a week. A typical week's training during this period should include:

- one long stamina run of 8 to 11 miles at 9:10 to 9:30 per mile
- one controlled-pace run of 4 to 8 miles at 8:50 to 9:20 per mile
- two endurance workouts on the track consisting of *one* of the following per workout:

  - 12 × 110 yards in 23 seconds, with a 330-yard recovery in between
  - 6 × 220 yards in 47 seconds, with a 440-yard recovery in between
  - 6 × 440 yards in 97 seconds, with a 440-yard recovery in between
  - 3 × 880 yards in 3 minutes 50 seconds, with an 880-yard recovery in between
  - 2 × 1 mile in 8 minutes, with an 880-yard recovery in between

- three days of easy running (4 to 6 miles) at 9:30 to 10:00 per mile

Select one short-distance (110 to 440 yards) and one medium-distance (880 yards to 1 mile) endurance workout in each week's training.

Substitute 3 competitive efforts (5K to 20K) for 3 of the "easy running" days during the first eight-week period of 10K training.

FINAL EIGHT-WEEK SCHEDULE

"Easy running" in this schedule is 9:30 to 10:00 per mile.

1st Week

Day

1. 10 miles easy running
2. 6 × 440 in :93 — 440 R
3. 5 miles easy running
4. 2 × 2 miles in 16:30 — 1-mile R
5. 4 miles easy running
6. 4 miles incorporating 3 miles in 25:00
7. 6 miles incorporating 3 miles in 25:00

2nd Week

Day

1. 8 miles easy running
2. 8 × 220 in :46 — 440 R
3. 5 miles easy running
4. 3 × 1 mile in 7:50 — 880 R
5. 3 miles easy running
6. Rest day
7. Competitive effort: 5K to 20K

3rd Week

Day

1. 4–7 miles easy running
2. 6 × 440 in 1:40 — 440 R
3. 6 miles incorporating 2 × 1 mile in 7:50
4. 3 miles easy running
5. Rest day
6. 5 miles easy running
7. 6 miles incorporating 3 miles in 23:45

4th Week

Day

1. 9 miles easy running
2. 10 × 110 in :23 — 110 R
3. 5 miles easy running
4. 3 × 880 in 3:50 — 880 R
5. 3 miles easy running
6. Rest day
7. Competitive effort: 5K to 15K

5th Week

Day

1. 4–7 miles easy running
2. 6 × 220 in :47 — 440 R
3. 5 miles easy running
4. 4 miles easy running
5. 3 × 1 mile in 7:50 — 880 R
6. 3 miles easy running
7. 3 miles easy running

6th Week

Day

1. 10 miles in 87:30
2. 4 miles easy running
3. 6 × 440 in :96 — 440 R
4. 5 miles easy running
5. 3 miles easy running
6. Rest day
7. Competitive effort: 5K to 15K

7th Week

Day

1 4–6 miles easy running
2 5 × 440 in 1:40 — 440 R
3 4 miles easy running
4 10 miles in 87:30
5 4 miles easy running
6 Rest day
7 6 miles incorporating 2 × 1 mile in 7:50

8th Week

Day

1 6 miles easy running
2 8 × 220 in :46 — 440 R
3 5 miles easy running
4 4 miles easy running
5 Rest day
6 Rest day
7 51-minute 30-second 10K

J. R. Shannon, CEO (Photograph by Bruce Glikin)

The 54-Minute 10K

You are ready to train for a 54-minute 10K if you can run:

220 yards in 42.5 seconds
440 yards in 91.5 seconds
1 mile in 7 minutes 50 seconds

To run 10K in 54 minutes you need to average 8:44 per mile.

In the first eight weeks of training for this event, you should establish a base of 30 to 40 miles a week. A typical week's training during this period should include:

- one long stamina run of 7 to 10 miles at 9:30 to 9:45 per mile
- one controlled-pace run of 4 to 7 miles at 9:10 to 9:25 per mile
- two endurance workouts on the track consisting of *one* of the following per workout:

    - 10 × 110 yards in 23 seconds, with a 330-yard recovery in between
    - 6 × 220 yards in 48 seconds, with a 440-yard recovery in between
    - 5 × 440 yards in 99 seconds, with a 440-yard recovery in between
    - 3 × 880 yards in 3 minutes 55 seconds, with an 880-yard recovery in between
    - 2 × 1 mile in 8 minutes 10 seconds, with an 880-yard recovery in between

- three days of easy running (3 to 5 miles) at 9:45 to 10:15 per mile

Select one short-distance (110 to 440 yards) and one medium-distance (880 yards to 1 mile) endurance workout in each week's training.

Substitute 3 competitive efforts (5K to 15K) for 3 of the "easy running" days during the first six-week period of 10K training.

FINAL SIX-WEEK SCHEDULE

"Easy running" in this schedule is 9:45 to 10:15 per mile.

1st Week

Day

1   8 miles easy running
2   6 × 440 in :96 — 440 R
3   5 miles easy running
4   2 × 2 miles in 17:30 — 1-mile R
5   3 miles easy running
6   4 miles incorporating 1 mile in 8:15
7   6 miles incorporating 3 miles in 26:15

2nd Week

Day

1   8 miles easy running
2   6 × 220 in :47 — 440 R
3   4 miles easy running
4   2 × 1 mile in 8:15 — 880 R
5   3 miles easy running
6   Rest day
7   Competitive effort: 5K to 15K

3rd Week

Day

1   3–5 miles easy running
2   5 × 440 in 1:40 — 440 R
3   4 miles incorporating 2 × 1 mile in 8:15
4   3 miles easy running
5   3 miles easy running
6   Rest day
7   7 miles incorporating 3 miles in 26:15

4th Week

Day

1   10 miles easy running
2   8 × 110 in :23 — 330 R
3   5 miles easy running
4   3 × 880 in 3:55 — 880 R
5   3 miles easy running
6   Rest day
7   Competitive effort: 5K to 15K

5th Week

Day

1   4 miles easy running
2   5 × 440 in 1:40 — 440 R
3   4 miles easy running
4   8 miles in 72:00
5   4 miles easy running
6   Rest day
7   6 miles incorporating 2 × 1 mile in 8:15

6th Week

Day

1   6 miles easy running
2   8 × 220 in :48 — 440 R
3   5 miles easy running
4   4 miles easy running
5   Rest day
6   Rest day
7   54-minute 10K

The 58-Minute 10K

You are ready to train for a 58-minute 10K if you can run:

220 yards in 46 seconds
440 yards in 1 minute 45 seconds
1 mile in 8 minutes 30 seconds

To run a 10K in 58 minutes you need to average 9:23 per mile.

In the first eight weeks of training for this event, you should establish a base of 25 to 35 miles a week. A typical week's training during this period should include:

- one long stamina run of 5 to 8 miles at 10:00 to 10:30 per mile
- one controlled-pace run of 3 to 6 miles at 9:30 to 9:45 per mile
- two endurance workouts on the track consisting of *one* of the following per workout:

    - 10 × 110 yards in 24 seconds, with a 330-yard recovery in between
    - 5 × 220 yards in 50 seconds, with a 440-yard recovery in between
    - 4 × 440 yards in 2 minutes, with a 440-yard recovery in between
    - 2 × 880 yards in 4 minutes 15 seconds, with an 880-yard recovery in between
    - 1 × 1 mile in 8 minutes 50 seconds

- two days of easy running (3 to 4 miles) at 10:00 to 10:30 per mile
- one rest day

Select one short-distance (110 to 440 yards) and one medium-distance (880 yards to 1 mile) endurance workout in each week's training.

Substitute 3 competitive efforts (5K to 15K) for 3 of the "easy running" days during the first six-week period of 10K training.

FINAL SIX-WEEK SCHEDULE

"Easy running" in this schedule is 10:15 to 10:45 per mile.

1st Week

Day

1. 10 miles easy running
2. 5 × 440 in 1:52 — 440 R
3. 4 miles easy running
4. 2 × 2 miles in 18:45 — 1-mile R
5. 4 miles easy running
6. 3 miles incorporating 1 mile in 9:00
7. 5 miles incorporating 3 miles in 28:00

2nd Week

Day

1. 7 miles easy running
2. 10 × 110 in :23 — 330 R
3. 4 miles easy running
4. 2 × 1 mile in 9:00 — 880 R
5. Rest day
6. Rest day
7. Competitive effort: 5K to 15K

3rd Week

Day

1. 2–4 miles easy running
2. 6 × 220 in :49 — 440 R
3. Rest day
4. 4 miles easy running
5. 7 miles in 69:00
6. Rest day
7. 5 miles incorporating 3 miles in 28:15

4th Week

Day

1. 9 miles easy running
2. 4 miles easy running
3. 2 × ¾ mile in 6:45 — 1-mile R
4. 4 miles easy running
5. Rest day
6. Rest day
7. Competitive effort: 5K to 15K

5th Week

Day

1 4 miles easy running
2 4 × 440 in 1:52 — 440 R
3 4 miles easy running
4 7 miles in 70:00
5 4 miles easy running
6 Rest day
7 5 miles incorporating 2 × 1 mile in 9:00

6th Week

Day

1 5 miles easy running
2 6 × 220 in :49 — 440 R
3 4 miles easy running
4 4 miles easy running
5 Rest day
6 Rest day
7 58-minute 10K

Dutch Teneyck, electrical design engineer. (Photograph by Carolyn Banks)

CHAPTER 8

Schedules for the Marathons

The 2-Hour 25-Minute Marathon

You are ready to train for a 2-hour 25-minute marathon if you can run:

> *1 mile in 4 minutes 30 seconds*
> *10K in 31 minutes 30 seconds*

To run a 2-hour 25-minute marathon you need to average 5:32 per mile.

In the first ten weeks of training for this event, you should establish a base of 65 to 80 miles a week. A typical week's training during this period should include:

- one long stamina run of 16 to 20 miles at 6:40 to 7:15 per mile
- one controlled-pace run of 6 to 10 miles at 5:32 to 5:40 per mile
- two endurance workouts on the track consisting of *one* of the following per workout:

  . 20 × 110 yards in 17 seconds, with a 330-yard recovery in between
  . 16 × 440 yards in 75 to 80 seconds, with a 440-yard recovery in between

- 5 to 8 × 880 yards in 2 minutes 35 seconds, with a 440-yard recovery in between
- 4 × 1 mile in 5 minutes 15 seconds, with an 880-yard recovery in between
- 3 × 1.5 miles in 8 minutes 15 seconds, with an 880-yard recovery in between

• three days of easy running (10 to 14 miles) at 6:40 to 7:15 per mile

Select one short-distance (110 to 440 yards) and one medium-distance (880 yards to 1.5 miles) endurance workout in each week's training.

During the first ten-week training period, you should attempt 4 races at distances of 8K to 20K. These races should replace an "easy running" day.

FINAL TEN-WEEK SCHEDULE

"Easy running" in this schedule is 6:15 to 7:00 per mile. (After any race, if necessary, add 30 seconds to 1 minute per mile to your "easy running" pace.)

1st Week

Day

1 15 miles easy running
2 12 × 440 in :76 — 220 R
3 10 miles easy running
4 12 miles incorporating 10 miles in 56:30
5 10 miles easy running
6 6 miles easy running
7 18 miles at 6:10–6:20 per mile

2nd Week

Day

1 15 miles easy running
2 25 × 110 in :17 — 110 R
3 10 miles easy running
4 6–10 × 440 in :69 — 440 R
5 10 miles easy running
6 6 miles easy running
7 20 miles in 2:01:40–2:05:00

3rd Week

Day

1 15 miles easy running
2 6 × 1 mile in 5:20–5:26 — 440 R
3 10 miles easy running
4 12–16 × 220 in :35–:37 — 220 R
5 6 miles easy running
6 Rest day
7 Competitive effort: 15K to 25K

4th Week

Day

1 9–14 miles easy running
2 6 miles easy running
3 16 × 220 in :36–:38 — 110 R
4 10 miles incorporating 2 × 2 miles in 10:30
5 10 miles easy running
6 5 miles easy running
7 23 miles easy running

5th Week

Day

1 10 miles easy running
2 4 × 1 mile in 5:10 — 440 R
3 10 miles easy running
4 2 × 2 miles in 10:00–10:15 — 880 R
5 10 miles easy running
6 Rest day
7 20 miles at 7:00 per mile

6th Week

Day

1 18 miles incorporating 3 × 3 miles in 16:00–16:30
2 10 miles easy running
3 6 miles incorporating 3 miles in 15:30–16:00
4 10 miles easy running
5 4 × 880 in 2:20–2:25 — 880 R
6 3 miles easy running
7 Competitive effort: 10 miles–30K

7th Week

Day

1 10 miles easy running
2 6 miles easy running
3 Rest day
4 3 × 2 miles in 10:40–11:00 — 880 R
5 10 miles easy running
6 10 miles in 58:30
7 15 miles easy running

8th Week

Day

1 20 miles at 7:00 per mile
2 2 × 2 miles in 10:10–10:20 — 880 R
3 10 miles easy running
4 20 × 440 in :76 — 220 R
5 10 miles easy running
6 Rest day
7 24 miles in 2:36:00

9th Week

Day

1 12 miles easy running
2 12 miles incorporating 3 miles in 15:30
3 20 × 110 in :18 — 110 R
4 10 miles easy running
5 12 miles incorporating 10 miles in 56:30
6 6 miles easy running
7 18 miles easy running

10th Week

Day

1 8 miles easy running
2 5 miles easy running
3 3 × 1 mile in 5:30 — 880 R
4 5 miles easy running
5 Rest day
6 Rest day or 3 miles easy running
7 2-hour 25-minute marathon

Robert Gray, investor. (Photograph by Bruce Glikin)

The 2-Hour 35-Minute Marathon

You are ready to train for a 2-hour 35-minute marathon if you can run:

1 mile in 4 minutes 50 seconds
10K in 33 minutes 30 seconds

To run a 2-hour 35-minute marathon you need to average 5:54 per mile.

In the first ten weeks of training for this event, you should establish a base of 65 to 80 miles a week. A typical week's training during this period should include:

- one long stamina run of 16 to 20 miles at 6:55 to 7:40 per mile
- one controlled-pace run of 6 to 10 miles at 5:55 to 6:05 per mile
- two endurance workouts on the track consisting of *one* of the following per workout:

  - 20 × 110 yards in 18 seconds, with a 330-yard recovery in between
  - 12 to 16 × 440 yards in 80 seconds, with a 440-yard recovery in between
  - 5 to 8 × 880 yards in 2 minutes 45 seconds, with an 880-yard recovery in between
  - 3 × 1 mile in 5 minutes 20 seconds, with an 880-yard recovery in between
  - 2 × 1.5 miles in 8 minutes 40 seconds, with an 880-yard recovery in between

- three days of easy running (10 to 14 miles) at 6:50 to 7:40 per mile

Select one short-distance (110 to 440 yards) and one medium-distance (880 yards to 1.5 miles) endurance workout in each week's training.

During the first ten-week training period, you should attempt 4 races at distances of 8K to 20K. These races should replace an "easy running" day.

FINAL TEN-WEEK SCHEDULE

"Easy running" in this schedule is 6:40 to 7:15 per mile.

1st Week

Day

1 15 miles easy running
2 12 × 440 in :80 — 110 R
3 10 miles easy running
4 12 miles incorporating 10 miles in 61:30
5 3 × 1 mile in 5:30 — 440 R
6 8 miles easy running
7 16 miles at 6:20–6:30 per mile

2nd Week

Day

1 15 miles easy running
2 16 × 220 in :38 — 220 R
3 10 miles easy running
4 8 × 440 in :70 — 440 R
5 10 miles easy running
6 Rest day
7 22 miles at 6:20–6:30 per mile

3rd Week

Day

1 12 miles easy running
2 6 × ¾ mile in 4:05 — 660 R
3 12 miles easy running
4 10 miles incorporating 2 × 2 miles in 11:00–11:20
5 10 miles easy running
6 Rest day
7 Competitive effort: 15K to 25K

4th Week

Day

1 10 miles easy running
2 6 miles easy running
3 25 × 110 in :18 — 110 R
4 12 miles easy running
5 10 × 440 in :80 — 220 R
6 10 miles easy running
7 15 miles in 1:37:30

5th Week

Day

1 22 miles easy running
2 10 × 220 in :36 — 220 R
3 10 miles easy running
4 2 × 2 miles in 10:30 — 880 R
5 6 miles easy running
6 Rest day
7 Competitive effort: 10K to 25K

6th Week

Day

1 18 miles easy running
2 6 miles easy running
3 4 × 880 in 2:35 — 660 R
4 10 miles easy running
5 10 miles easy running
6 6 miles easy running
7 22 miles easy running

7th Week

Day

1 12 miles incorporating 2 × 3 miles in 17:30
2 6 miles easy running
3 8 × 880 in 2:45 — 660 R
4 10 miles easy running
5 6 miles incorporating 2 miles in 11:00
6 Rest day
7 Competitive effort:10K to 20K

8th Week

Day

1 14–20 miles easy running
2 12 × 440 in :78 — 440 R
3 10 miles easy running
4 25 × 110 in :18 — 110 R
5 6 miles easy running
6 Rest day
7 22 miles easy running

9th Week

Day

1 12 miles incorporating 10 miles in 58:30
2 8 × 440 in :75 — 440 R
3 10 miles easy running
4 10 miles incorporating 2 × 2 miles in 11:00
5 6 miles easy running
6 Rest day
7 18 miles easy running

10th Week

Day

1 12 miles easy running
2 6 miles easy running
3 6 × 220 in :36 — 440 R
4 6 miles easy running
5 Rest day
6 Rest day or 3 miles easy running
7 2-hour 35-minute marathon

Michael Carnes, business vice-president. (Photograph by Bruce Glikin)

The 2-Hour 45-Minute Marathon

> *You are ready to train for a 2-hour 45-minute marathon if you can run:*
>
> *1 mile in 5 minutes 5 seconds*
> *10K in 35 minutes 45 seconds*
>
> *To run a 2-hour 45-minute marathon you need to average 6:17 per mile.*

In the first ten weeks of training for this event, you should establish a base of 60 to 75 miles a week. A typical week's training during this period should include:

- one long stamina run of 15 to 19 miles at 7:10 to 7:55 per mile
- one controlled-pace run of 6 to 10 miles at 6:10 to 6:30 per mile
- two endurance workouts on the track consisting of *one* of the following per workout:

  - 12 × 220 yards in 38 seconds, with a 440-yard recovery in between
  - 12 × 440 yards in 82 to 84 seconds, with a 440-yard recovery in between
  - 5 × 880 yards in 2 minutes 50 seconds, with a 440-yard recovery in between
  - 3 × 1 mile in 5 minutes 50 seconds, with a 440-yard recovery in between

- three days of easy running (9 to 13 miles) at 7:10 to 7:55 per mile

Select one short-distance (220 to 440 yards) and one medium-distance (880 yards to 1 mile) endurance workout in each week's training.

During the first ten-week training period, you should attempt 4 races at distances of 8K to 20K. These races should replace an "easy running" day.

FINAL TEN-WEEK SCHEDULE

"Easy running" in this schedule is 7:10 to 7:55 per mile.

1st Week

Day

1 15 miles easy running
2 12 × 440 in :82–:84 — 220 R
3 10 miles easy running
4 12 miles incorporating 10 miles in 65:00
5 7 miles easy running
6 3 × 1 mile in 5:45 — 880 R
7 10 miles easy running

2nd Week

Day

1 16 miles at 6:50 per mile
2 10 × 220 in :38 — 440 R
3 12 miles easy running
4 5 × 880 in 2:50 — 440 R
5 10 miles easy running
6 Rest day
7 21 miles at 7:00 per mile

3rd Week

Day

1 10 miles easy running
2 10 × 440 in :80 — 440 R
3 12 miles easy running
4 10 miles at 7:00 per mile
5 10 miles easy running
6 4 miles easy running
7 Competitive effort: 15K to 25K

4th Week

Day

1 6 miles easy running
2 13 miles easy running
3 20 × 110 in :18 — 330 R
4 10 miles easy running

5 8 × 440 in :78 — 440 R
6 6 miles easy running
7 21 miles easy running

5th Week

Day

1 10 miles incorporating 2 × 2 miles in 12:00
2 6 miles easy running
3 10 miles easy running
4 4 × 1 mile in 5:45 — 880 R
5 6 miles easy running
6 Rest day
7 Competitive effort: 10K to 25K

6th Week

Day

1 9–13 miles easy running
2 10 × 220 in :38 — 440 R
3 12 miles easy running
4 6 miles easy running
5 12 miles incorporating 10 miles in 65:00
6 Rest day
7 21 miles easy running

7th Week

Day

1 10 miles incorporating 2 × 2 miles in 12:00
2 8 miles easy running
3 16 × 440 in :88 — 110 R
4 12 miles easy running
5 Rest day
6 6 miles easy running
7 Competitive effort:10K to 20K

8th Week

Day

1 9–16 miles easy running
2 16 × 220 in :40 — 110 R
3 12 miles easy running
4 10 miles in 67:30
5 6 miles easy running
6 6 miles easy running
7 22 miles easy running

9th Week

Day

1 12 miles incorporating 10 miles in 62:30
2 6 miles easy running
3 6 × 880 in 2:45 — 660 R
4 12 miles easy running
5 6 miles easy running
6 9 miles incorporating 2 × 2 miles in 11:45
7 14 miles easy running

10th Week

Day

1 6 miles easy running
2 3 × 880 in 2:45 — 880 R
3 6 miles easy running
4 6 miles easy running
5 Rest day
6 Rest day or 3 miles easy running
7 2-hour 45-minute marathon

Edward Castro, systems technician. (Photograph by Bruce Glikin)

The 2-Hour 55-Minute Marathon

You are ready to train for a 2-hour 55-minute marathon if you can run:

1 mile in 5 minutes 26 seconds
10K in 37 minutes 45 seconds

To run a 2-hour 55-minute marathon you need to average 6:40 per mile.

In the first ten weeks of training for this event, you should establish a base of 60 to 75 miles a week. A typical week's training during this period should include:

- one long stamina run of 15 to 19 miles at 7:35 to 8:15 per mile
- one controlled-pace run of 6 to 10 miles at 6:40 to 7:10 per mile
- two endurance workouts on the track consisting of *one* of the following per workout:

  - 16 × 110 yards in 18 seconds, with a 330-yard recovery in between
  - 12 × 440 yards in 85 seconds, with a 440-yard recovery in between
  - 5 × 880 yards in 2 minutes 56 seconds, with a 440-yard recovery in between
  - 3 × 1 mile in 6 minutes, with a 440-yard recovery in between

- three days of easy running (8 to 12 miles) at 7:35 to 8:15 per mile

Select one short-distance (110 to 440 yards) and one medium-distance (880 yards to 1 mile) endurance workout in each week's training.

During the first ten-week training period, you should attempt 4 races at distances of 8K to 20K. These races should replace an "easy running" day.

FINAL TEN-WEEK SCHEDULE

"Easy running" in this schedule is 7:35 to 8:15 per mile.

1st Week

Day

1 15 miles easy running
2 12 × 440 in :84–:86 — 220 R
3 10 miles easy running
4 10 miles in 70:00
5 6 miles easy running
6 3 × 1 mile in 5:52 — 880 R
7 8 miles easy running

2nd Week

Day

1 16 miles at 7:00 per mile
2 16 × 110 in :18 — 220 R
3 10 miles easy running
4 5 × 880 in 3:00 — 440 R
5 6 miles easy running
6 4 miles easy running
7 21 miles at 7:15 per mile

3rd Week

Day

1 10 miles easy running
2 12–16 × 220 in :40–:42 — 220 R
3 12 miles easy running
4 10 miles incorporating 2 × 2 miles in 12:00
5 8 miles easy running
6 Rest day
7 Competitive effort: 10K to 25K

4th Week

Day

1 6–10 miles easy running
2 12 miles easy running
3 12 × 440 in :84 — 440 R
4 10 miles easy running
5 4 × 880 in 2:50 — 880 R
6 Rest day
7 21 miles easy running

5th Week

Day

1 10 miles incorporating 4 miles in 26:00
2 6 miles easy running
3 8 miles easy running
4 3 × 1 mile in 5:52 — 880 R
5 6 miles easy running
6 Rest day
7 Competitive effort: 10K to 25K

6th Week

Day

1 9–13 miles easy running
2 16 × 110 in :19 — 110 R
3 10 miles easy running
4 6 miles easy running
5 12 miles incorporating 10 miles in 66:30
6 Rest day
7 21 miles easy running

7th Week

Day

1 10 miles incorporating 2 × 1 mile in 5:50
2 6 miles easy running
3 12 × 440 in :90 — 220 R
4 13 miles easy running
5 5 miles easy running
6 Rest day
7 Competitive effort:10K to 20K

8th Week

Day

1 10–14 miles easy running
2 12 × 220 in :42 — 220 R
3 12 miles easy running
4 10 miles in 70:00
5 6 miles easy running
6 Rest day
7 22 miles easy running

9th Week

Day

1 6 miles easy running
2 12 miles incorporating 10 miles in 65:00
3 6 miles easy running
4 8 miles easy running
5 9 miles incorporating 2 × 2 miles in 12:00
6 7 miles easy running
7 14 miles easy running

10th Week

Day

1 6 miles easy running
2 5 × 440 in :82 — 440 R
3 6 miles easy running
4 5 miles easy running
5 Rest day
6 Rest day or 3 miles easy running
7 2-hour 55-minute marathon

Glenn Good, mortgage banker. (Photograph by Bruce Glikin)

The 3-Hour 5-Minute Marathon

You are ready to train for a 3-hour 5-minute marathon if you can run:

1 mile in 5 minutes 36 seconds
10K in 39 minutes 45 seconds

To run a 3-hour 5-minute marathon you need to average 7:03 per mile.

In the first ten weeks of training for this event, you should establish a base of 55 to 70 miles a week. A typical week's training during this period should include:

- one long stamina run of 14 to 18 miles at 7:55 to 8:35 per mile
- one controlled-pace run of 6 to 10 miles at 7:00 to 7:35 per mile
- two endurance workouts on the track consisting of *one* of the following per workout:

  - 16 × 110 yards in 19 seconds, with a 330-yard recovery in between
  - 10 × 440 yards in 92 seconds, with a 440-yard recovery in between
  - 4 to 6 × 880 yards in 3 minutes 5 seconds, with a 440-yard recovery in between
  - 3 × 1 mile in 6 minutes 15 seconds, with a 440-yard recovery in between

- three days of easy running (8 to 12 miles) at 7:55 to 8:35 per mile

Select one short-distance (110 to 440 yards) and one medium-distance (880 yards to 1 mile) endurance workout in each week's training.

During the first ten-week training period, you should attempt 4 races at distances of 8K to 20K. These races should replace an "easy running" day.

FINAL TEN-WEEK SCHEDULE

"Easy running" in this schedule is 7:55 to 8:35 per mile.

1st Week

Day

1. 15 miles easy running
2. 12 × 220 in :41–:43 — 220 R
3. 10 miles easy running
4. 6 miles easy running
5. 10 miles in 72:30
6. 6 miles easy running
7. 9 miles incorporating 3 × 1 mile in 6:15

2nd Week

Day

1. 17 miles easy running
2. 16 × 110 in :20 — 110 R
3. 8 miles easy running
4. 5 × 880 in 3:10 — 440 R
5. 5 miles easy running
6. Rest day
7. 21 miles at 8:00 per mile

3rd Week

Day

1. 10 miles easy running
2. 8 × 440 in :86 — 440 R
3. 6 miles easy running
4. 10 miles easy running
5. 7 miles easy running
6. Rest day
7. Competitive effort: 10K to 25K

4th Week

Day

1. 6–10 miles easy running
2. 10 miles easy running
3. 12 × 220 in :44 — 110 R
4. 10 miles easy running
5. 4 × 880 in 3:00 — 880 R
6. Rest day
7. 21 miles easy running

5th Week

Day

1. 9 miles incorporating 2 × 2 miles in 13:30
2. 6 miles easy running
3. 6 miles easy running
4. 10 miles incorporating 3 × 1 mile in 6:10
5. 6 miles easy running
6. Rest day
7. Competitive effort: 10K to 25K

6th Week

Day

1. 8–12 miles easy running
2. 16 × 110 in :20 — 110 R
3. 12 miles easy running
4. 5 miles easy running
5. 12 miles incorporating 10 miles in 68:30
6. Rest day
7. 20 miles easy running

7th Week

Day

1. 10 miles incorporating 3 × 1 mile in 6:10
2. 6 miles easy running
3. 16 × 220 in :43 — 220 R
4. 12 miles easy running
5. 6 miles easy running
6. Rest day
7. Competitive effort: 10K to 20K

8th Week

Day

1   9–13 miles easy running
2   16 × 110 in :19 — 330 R
3   10 miles easy running
4   10 miles in 72:30
5   6 miles easy running
6   Rest day
7   22 miles easy running

9th Week

Day

1   6 miles easy running
2   12 miles incorporating 10 miles in 67:30

3   5 miles easy running
4   8 miles easy running
5   9 miles incorporating 2 × 2 miles in 12:15
6   6 miles easy running
7   14 miles easy running

10th Week

Day

1   6 miles easy running
2   5 × 440 in :85 — 440 R
3   5 miles easy running
4   4 miles easy running
5   Rest day
6   Rest day or 3 miles easy running
7   3-hour 5-minute marathon

Bernard Rogers, architect. (Photograph by Bruce Glikin)

The 3-Hour 15-Minute Marathon

You are ready to train for a 3-hour 15-minute marathon if you can run:

1 mile in 5 minutes 58 seconds
10K in 42 minutes

To run a 3-hour 15-minute marathon you need to average 7:25 per mile.

In the first ten weeks of training for this event, you should establish a base of 50 to 65 miles a week. A typical week's training during this period should include:

- one long stamina run of 13 to 17 miles at 8:10 to 8:55 per mile
- one controlled-pace run of 5 to 8 miles at 7:15 to 7:45 per mile
- two endurance workouts on the track consisting of *one* of the following per workout:

  - 12 × 110 yards in 20 seconds, with a 330-yard recovery in between
  - 10 × 440 yards in 94 seconds, with a 440-yard recovery in between
  - 4 × 880 yards in 3 minutes 10 seconds, with a 440-yard recovery in between
  - 3 × 1 mile in 6 minutes 25 seconds, with a 440-yard recovery in between

- three days of easy running (8 to 12 miles) at 8:10 to 8:55 per mile

Select one short-distance (110 to 440 yards) and one medium-distance (880 yards to 1 mile) endurance workout in each week's training.

During the first ten-week training period, you should attempt 4 races at distances of 8K to 20K. These races should replace an "easy running" day.

FINAL TEN-WEEK SCHEDULE

"Easy running" in this schedule is 8:10 to 8:55 per mile.

1st Week

Day

1. 14 miles easy running
2. 10 × 440 in :90 — 440 R
3. 9 miles easy running
4. 6 miles easy running
5. 10 miles in 75:00
6. 6 miles easy running
7. 8 miles incorporating 3 × 1 mile in 6:25

2nd Week

Day

1. 16 miles easy running
2. 16 × 110 in :21 — 110 R
3. 7 miles easy running
4. 5 × 880 in 3:12 — 440 R
5. 5 miles easy running
6. Rest day
7. 21 miles at 8:15 per mile

3rd Week

Day

1. 9 miles easy running
2. 8 × 440 in :90 — 220 R
3. 10 miles easy running
4. 6 miles easy running
5. 6 miles easy running
6. Rest day
7. Competitive effort: 10K to 25K

4th Week

Day

1. 6–10 miles easy running
2. 9 miles easy running
3. 16 × 110 in :20 — 110 R
4. 10 miles easy running
5. 3 × ¾ mile in 4:50 — 880 R
6. Rest day
7. 21 miles easy running

5th Week

Day

1. 9 miles incorporating 2 × 2 miles in 13:45
2. 6 miles easy running
3. 6 miles easy running
4. 10 miles incorporating 3 × 1 mile in 6:20
5. Rest day
6. 4 miles easy running
7. Competitive effort: 10K to 25K

6th Week

Day

1. 7–10 miles easy running
2. 8 × 220 in :42 — 440 R
3. 12 miles easy running
4. 3 miles easy running
5. Rest day
6. 6 miles easy running
7. 20 miles easy running

7th Week

Day

1. 10 miles incorporating 4 miles in 27:30
2. 6 miles easy running
3. 16 × 220 in :45 — 110 R
4. 10 miles easy running
5. 6 miles easy running
6. Rest day
7. Competitive effort: 10K to 20K

8th Week

Day

1   9–13 miles easy running
2   8 × 330 in :64 — 330 R
3   8 miles easy running
4   10 miles in 75:00
5   6 miles easy running
6   Rest day
7   22 miles easy running

9th Week

Day

1   5 miles easy running
2   12 miles incorporating 10 miles in 69:30

3   6 miles easy running
4   6 miles easy running
5   9 miles incorporating 2 × 2 miles in 12:45
6   5 miles easy running
7   14 miles easy running

10th Week

Day

1   6 miles easy running
2   5 × 440 in :88 — 440 R
3   4 miles easy running
4   4 miles easy running
5   Rest day
6   Rest day
7   3-hour 15-minute marathon

Jackie Delaney, psychologist. (Photograph by Bruce Glikin)

The 3-Hour 25-Minute Marathon

You are ready to train for a 3-hour 25-minute marathon if you can run:

1 mile in 6 minutes 8 seconds
10K in 43 minutes 15 seconds

To run a 3-hour 25-minute marathon you need to average 7:48 per mile.

In the first ten weeks of training for this event, you should establish a base of 50 to 60 miles a week. A typical week's training during this period should include:

- one long stamina run of 13 to 17 miles at 8:30 to 9:00 per mile
- two endurance workouts on the track consisting of *one* of the following per workout:

  - 12 × 110 yards in 21 seconds, with a 330-yard recovery in between
  - 10 × 440 yards in 96 seconds, with a 440-yard recovery in between
  - 4 × 880 yards in 3 minutes 18 seconds, with a 440-yard recovery in between
  - 3 × 1 mile in 6 minutes 45 seconds, with a 440-yard recovery in between

- four days of easy running (7 to 11 miles) at 8:30 to 9:00 per mile

Select one short-distance (110 to 440 yards) and one medium-distance (880 yards to 1 mile) endurance workout in each week's training.

During the first ten-week training period, you should attempt 4 races at distances of 8K to 20K. These races should replace an "easy running" day.

FINAL TEN-WEEK SCHEDULE

"Easy running" in this schedule is 8:30 to 9:00 per mile.

1st Week

Day

1 14 miles easy running
2 10 × 440 in :95 — 440 R
3 9 miles easy running
4 6 miles easy running
5 10 miles in 77:30
6 4 miles easy running
7 7 miles incorporating 3 × 1 mile in 6:40

2nd Week

Day

1 16 miles easy running
2 8 × 220 in :43 — 440 R
3 7 miles easy running
4 5 × 880 in 3:18 — 440 R
5 5 miles easy running
6 Rest day
7 20 miles at 8:30 per mile

3rd Week

Day

1 8 miles easy running
2 8 × 440 in :92 — 440 R
3 7 miles easy running
4 10 miles easy running
5 6 miles easy running
6 Rest day
7 Competitive effort: 10K to 25K

4th Week

Day

1 6–10 miles easy running
2 9 miles easy running
3 16 × 110 in :21 — 110 R
4 10 miles easy running

5 3 × 880 in 3:15 — 880 R
6 Rest day
7 21 miles easy running

5th Week

Day

1 9 miles incorporating 2 × 2 miles in 14:00
2 6 miles easy running
3 5 miles easy running
4 10 miles incorporating 3 × 1 mile in 6:30
5 4 miles easy running
6 Rest day
7 Competitive effort: 10K to 25K

6th Week

Day

1 6–9 miles easy running
2 8 × 220 in :44 — 440 R
3 12 miles easy running
4 3 miles easy running
5 10 miles in 78:00
6 Rest day
7 20 miles easy running

7th Week

Day

1 10 miles incorporating 4 miles in 28:30
2 6 miles easy running
3 12 × 220 in :45 — 220 R
4 10 miles easy running
5 5 miles easy running
6 Rest day
7 21 miles easy running

8th Week

Day

1 8–12 miles easy running
2 6 × 440 in :93 — 440 R
3 7 miles easy running
4 10 miles in 77:30
5 5 miles easy running
6 Rest day
7 21 miles easy running

9th Week

Day

1 5 miles easy running
2 12 miles incorporating 10 miles in 75:00
3 6 miles easy running
4 6 miles easy running
5 8 miles incorporating 2 × 2 miles in 13:20
6 5 miles easy running
7 13 miles easy running

10th Week

Day

1 6 miles easy running
2 5 × 440 in :90 — 440 R
3 5 miles easy running
4 4 miles easy running
5 Rest day
6 Rest day
7 3-hour 25-minute marathon

Larry Skelton, mortgage banker. (Photograph by Bruce Glikin)

The 3-Hour 35-Minute Marathon

You are ready to train for a 3-hour 35-minute marathon if you can run:

1 mile in 6 minutes 32 seconds
10K in 46 minutes

To run a 3-hour 35-minute marathon you need to average 8:11 per mile.

In the first ten weeks of training for this event, you should establish a base of 50 to 60 miles a week. A typical week's training during this period should include:

- one long stamina run of 13 to 17 miles at 8:50 to 9:20 per mile
- two endurance workouts on the track consisting of *one* of the following per workout:

  - 12 × 110 yards in 22 seconds, with a 330-yard recovery in between
  - 10 × 440 yards in 98 seconds, with a 440-yard recovery in between
  - 4 × 880 yards in 3 minutes 26 seconds, with a 440-yard recovery in between
  - 3 × 1 mile in 7 minutes 5 seconds, with a 440-yard recovery in between

- four days of easy running (7 to 11 miles) at 8:50 to 9:20 per mile

Select one short-distance (110 to 440 yards) and one medium-distance (880 yards to 1 mile) endurance workout in each week's training.

During the first ten-week training period, you should attempt 3 or 4 races at distances of 8K to 20K. These races should replace an "easy running" day.

FINAL TEN-WEEK SCHEDULE

"Easy running" in this schedule is 8:50 to 9:20 per mile.

1st Week

Day

1 14 miles easy running
2 10 × 440 in :97 — 440 R
3 9 miles easy running
4 6 miles easy running
5 10 miles in 80:00
6 4 miles easy running
7 7 miles incorporating 3 × 1 mile in 6:50

2nd Week

Day

1 15 miles easy running
2 6 × 220 in :44 — 440 R
3 7 miles easy running
4 4 × 880 in 3:25 — 440 R
5 5 miles easy running
6 Rest day
7 20 miles at 8:45 per mile

3rd Week

Day

1 7 miles easy running
2 8 × 440 in :94 — 440 R
3 7 miles easy running
4 10 miles easy running
5 6 miles easy running
6 Rest day
7 Competitive effort: 10K to 25K

4th Week

Day

1 6–10 miles easy running
2 9 miles easy running
3 16 × 110 in :22 — 110 R
4 10 miles easy running
5 3 × 880 in 3:20 — 880 R
6 Rest day
7 21 miles easy running

5th Week

Day

1 8 miles incorporating 2 × 2 miles in 14:20
2 6 miles easy running
3 5 miles easy running
4 10 miles incorporating 3 × 1 mile in 6:50
5 3 miles easy running
6 Rest day
7 Competitive effort: 10K to 25K

6th Week

Day

1 6 miles easy running
2 8 × 220 in :45 — 440 R
3 12 miles easy running
4 3 miles easy running
5 10 miles in 77:30
6 Rest day
7 20 miles easy running

7th Week

Day

1 10 miles incorporating 4 miles in 31:00
2 6 miles easy running
3 10 × 220 in :47 — 220 R
4 8 miles easy running
5 5 miles easy running
6 Rest day
7 Competitive effort:10K to 20K

8th Week

Day

1 8–12 miles easy running
2 12 × 110 in :21 — 220 R
3 6 miles easy running
4 10 miles in 77:30
5 4 miles easy running
6 Rest day
7 21 miles easy running

9th Week

Day

1 3 miles easy running
2 12 miles incorporating 10 miles in 80:00
3 5 miles easy running
4 5 miles easy running
5 7 miles incorporating 2 × 2 miles in 13:50
6 4 miles easy running
7 13 miles easy running

10th Week

Day

1 5 miles easy running
2 5 × 440 in :92 — 440 R
3 5 miles easy running
4 4 miles easy running
5 Rest day
6 Rest day
7 3-hour 35-minute marathon

Ilona Klar, independent businesswoman. (Photograph by Bruce Glikin)

The 3-Hour 45-Minute Marathon

You are ready to train for a 3-hour 45-minute marathon if you can run:

1 mile in 6 minutes 55 seconds
10K in 48 minutes 30 seconds

To run a 3-hour 45-minute marathon you need to average 8:34 per mile.

In the first ten weeks of training for this event, you should establish a base of 50 to 55 miles a week. A typical week's training during this period should include:

- one long stamina run of 12 to 16 miles at 9:15 to 10:00 per mile
- two endurance workouts on the track consisting of *one* of the following per workout:

  - 12 × 110 yards in 23 seconds, with a 330-yard recovery in between
  - 8 × 440 yards in 1 minute 40 seconds, with a 440-yard recovery in between
  - 4 × 880 yards in 3 minutes 35 seconds, with an 880-yard recovery in between
  - 3 × 1 mile in 7 minutes 35 seconds, with an 880-yard recovery in between

- four days of easy running (7 to 10 miles) at 9:15 to 10:00 per mile

Select one short-distance (110 to 440 yards) and one medium-distance (880 yards to 1 mile) endurance workout in each week's training.

During the first ten-week training period, you should attempt 3 or 4 races at distances of 8K to 20K. These races should replace an "easy running" day.

FINAL TEN-WEEK SCHEDULE

"Easy running" in this schedule is 9:15 to 10:00 per mile.

1st Week

Day

1. 14 miles easy running
2. 8 × 440 in :99 — 440 R
3. 9 miles easy running
4. 5 miles easy running
5. 10 miles in 82:30
6. 3 miles easy running
7. 6 miles incorporating 3 × 1 mile in 7:15

2nd Week

Day

1. 14 miles easy running
2. 6 × 220 in :46 — 440 R
3. 6 miles easy running
4. 4 × 880 in 3:30 — 880 R
5. 5 miles easy running
6. Rest day
7. 20 miles at 9:05 per mile

3rd Week

Day

1. 5 miles easy running
2. 12 × 110 in :22 — 330 R
3. 7 miles easy running
4. 10 miles easy running
5. 4 miles easy running
6. Rest day
7. Competitive effort: 10K to 25K

4th Week

Day

1. 6–10 miles easy running
2. 7 miles easy running
3. 8 × 220 in :46 — 220 R
4. 10 miles easy running
5. 3 × 880 in 3:30 — 880 R
6. Rest day
7. 21 miles easy running

5th Week

Day

1. 6 miles incorporating 2 × 1 mile in 7:10
2. 6 miles easy running
3. 6 miles easy running
4. 12 miles easy running
5. 3 miles easy running
6. Rest day
7. Competitive effort: 10K to 25K

6th Week

Day

1. 5 miles easy running
2. 12 × 110 in :22 — 330 R
3. 10 miles easy running
4. Rest day
5. 10 miles in 80:00
6. Rest day
7. 20 miles easy running

7th Week

Day

1. 9 miles incorporating 3 miles in 23:00
2. 6 miles easy running
3. 6 × 220 in :48 — 220 R
4. 6 miles incorporating 2 miles in 15:00
5. 4 miles easy running
6. Rest day
7. Competitive effort:10K to 20K

8th Week

Day

1 6 miles easy running
2 10 × 110 in :22 — 330 R
3 10 miles in 79:00
4 5 miles easy running
5 3 miles easy running
6 Rest day
7 19 miles easy running

9th Week

Day

1 3 miles easy running
2 12 miles incorporating 10 miles in 80:00
3 5 miles easy running
4 5 miles easy running
5 6 miles incorporating 2 × 2 miles in 14:40
6 3 miles easy running
7 12 miles easy running

10th Week

Day

1 6 miles easy running
2 5 × 440 in :96 — 440 R
3 4 miles easy running
4 4 miles easy running
5 Rest day
6 Rest day
7 3-hour 45-minute marathon

Roy H. Cullen, energy exploration executive. (Photograph by Bruce Glikin)

The 3-Hour 55-Minute Marathon

You are ready to train for a 3-hour 55-minute marathon if you can run:

1 mile in 7 minutes 12 seconds
10K in 50 minutes 45 seconds

To run a 3-hour 55-minute marathon you need to average 8:58 per mile.

In the first ten weeks of training for this event, you should establish a base of 45 to 50 miles a week. A typical week's training during this period should include:

- one long stamina run of 12 to 15 miles at 9:40 to 10:20 per mile
- two endurance workouts on the track consisting of *one* of the following per workout:

  - 12 × 110 yards in 23 seconds, with a 330-yard recovery in between
  - 8 × 440 yards in 1 minute 45 seconds, with a 440-yard recovery in between
  - 4 × 880 yards in 3 minutes 40 seconds, with a 440-yard recovery in between
  - 3 × 1 mile in 7 minutes 45 seconds, with an 880-yard recovery in between

- four days of easy running (7 to 10 miles) at 9:40 to 10:20 per mile

Select one short-distance (110 to 440 yards) and one medium-distance (880 yards to 1 mile) endurance workout in each week's training.

During the first ten-week training period, you should attempt 3 or 4 races at distances of 8K to 20K. These races should replace an "easy running" day.

FINAL TEN-WEEK SCHEDULE

"Easy running" in this schedule is 9:40 to 10:20 per mile.

1st Week

Day

1 13 miles easy running
2 8 × 440 in 1:42 — 440 R
3 8 miles easy running
4 5 miles easy running
5 10 miles in 87:30
6 3 miles easy running
7 6 miles incorporating 3 × 1 mile in 7:35

2nd Week

Day

1 14 miles easy running
2 6 × 220 in :47 — 440 R
3 5 miles easy running
4 4 × 880 in 3:40 — 880 R
5 4 miles easy running
6 Rest day
7 20 miles at 9:30 per mile

3rd Week

Day

1 4 miles easy running
2 10 × 110 in :22 — 330 R
3 9 miles easy running
4 6 miles easy running
5 4 miles easy running
6 Rest day
7 Competitive effort: 10K to 25K

4th Week

Day

1 6–9 miles easy running
2 6 miles easy running
3 8 × 220 in :47 — 220 R
4 10 miles easy running
5 2 × 880 in 3:35 — ¾-mile R
6 Rest day
7 20 miles easy running

5th Week

Day

1 6 miles incorporating 2 × 1 mile in 7:30
2 5 miles easy running
3 5 miles easy running
4 12 miles easy running
5 3 miles easy running
6 Rest day
7 Competitive effort: 10K to 25K

6th Week

Day

1 4 miles easy running
2 10 × 110 in :23 — 330 R
3 8 miles easy running
4 Rest day
5 10 miles in 82:30
6 Rest day
7 18 miles easy running

7th Week

Day

1 8 miles incorporating 3 miles in 24:00
2 5 miles easy running
3 6 × 220 in :48 — 440 R
4 5 miles incorporating 2 miles in 15:30
5 3 miles easy running
6 Rest day
7 Competitive effort: 10K to 20K

8th Week

Day

1. 4 miles easy running
2. 10 × 220 in :23 — 330 R
3. 10 miles in 81:00
4. 4 miles easy running
5. 3 miles easy running
6. Rest day
7. 19 miles easy running

9th Week

Day

1. 3 miles easy running
2. 12 miles incorporating 10 miles in 82:30
3. 5 miles easy running
4. 3 miles easy running
5. 6 miles incorporating 2 × 2 miles in 15:30
6. 3 miles easy running
7. 10 miles easy running

10th Week

Day

1. 5 miles easy running
2. 5 × 440 in :98 — 440 R
3. 4 miles easy running
4. 3 miles easy running
5. Rest day
6. Rest day
7. 3-hour 55-minute marathon

Jeanie Hoepfel, cardiac rehabilitation nurse. (Photograph by Bruce Glikin)

The 4-Hour 5-Minute Marathon

You are ready to train for a 4-hour 5-minute marathon if you can run:

1 mile in 7 minutes 30 seconds
10K in 53 minutes

To run a 4-hour 5-minute marathon you need to average 9:20 per mile.

In the first ten weeks of training for this event, you should establish a base of 45 to 50 miles a week. A typical week's training during this period should include:

- one long stamina run of 12 to 15 miles at 10:00 to 10:45 per mile
- two endurance workouts on the track consisting of *one* of the following per workout:

  - 12 × 110 yards in 24 seconds, with a 330-yard recovery in between
  - 6 × 440 yards in 1 minute 48 seconds, with a 440-yard recovery in between
  - 4 × 880 yards in 3 minutes 45 seconds, with an 880-yard recovery in between
  - 3 × 1 mile in 8 minutes, with an 880-yard recovery in between

- four days of easy running (7 to 10 miles) at 10:00 to 10:45 per mile

Select one short-distance (110 to 440 yards) and one medium-distance (880 yards to 1 mile) endurance workout in each week's training.

During the first ten-week training period, you should attempt 3 or 4 races at distances of 8K to 20K. These races should replace an "easy running" day.

FINAL TEN-WEEK SCHEDULE

"Easy running" in this schedule is 10:00 to 10:45 per mile.

1st Week

Day

1 14 miles easy running
2 6 × 440 in 1:45 — 440 R
3 9 miles easy running
4 Rest day
5 10 miles in 87:30
6 3 miles easy running
7 6 miles incorporating 3 × 1 mile in 7:45

2nd Week

Day

1 13.1 miles easy running
2 6 × 220 in :48 — 440 R
3 6 miles easy running
4 3 × 880 in 3:45 — 880 R
5 5 miles easy running
6 Rest day
7 18 miles at 9:30 per mile

3rd Week

Day

1 5 miles easy running
2 12 × 110 in :23 — 220 R
3 6 miles easy running
4 8 miles easy running
5 4 miles easy running
6 Rest day
7 Competitive effort: 10K to 20K

4th Week

Day

1 5–8 miles easy running
2 6 miles easy running
3 8 × 220 in :48 — 220 R
4 8 miles easy running

5 2 × ¾ mile in 5:45 — ¾-mile R
6 Rest day
7 20 miles easy running

5th Week

Day

1 6 miles incorporating 1 mile in 7:45
2 6 miles easy running
3 6 miles easy running
4 10 miles easy running
5 3 miles easy running
6 Rest day
7 Competitive effort: 10K to 25K

6th Week

Day

1 5 miles easy running
2 10 × 110 in :23 — 330 R
3 10 miles easy running
4 Rest day
5 10 miles in 85:00 to 87:30
6 Rest day
7 18 miles easy running

7th Week

Day

1 9 miles incorporating 3 miles in 25:00
2 6 miles easy running
3 6 × 220 in :48 — 440 R
4 6 miles incorporating 2 miles in 15:40
5 3 miles easy running
6 Rest day
7 Competitive effort:10K to 20K

8th Week

Day

1 6 miles easy running
2 8 × 220 in :50 — 220 R
3 10 miles in 87:30
4 5 miles easy running
5 3 miles easy running
6 Rest day
7 18 miles easy running

9th Week

Day

1 3 miles easy running
2 12 miles incorporating 10 miles in 85:00
3 5 miles easy running
4 4 miles easy running
5 6 miles incorporating 2 × 1 mile in 7:50
6 3 miles easy running
7 12 miles easy running

10th Week

Day

1 6 miles easy running
2 5 × 440 in :98 — 440 R
3 4 miles easy running
4 4 miles easy running
5 Rest day
6 Rest day
7 4-hour 5-minute marathon

Carol Slocomb, symphony musician. (Photograph by Bruce Glikin)

The 4-Hour 25-Minute Marathon

> *You are ready to train for a 4-hour 25-minute marathon if you can run:*
>
> *1 mile in 8 minutes 5 seconds*
> *10K in 57 minutes 15 seconds*
>
> *To run a 4-hour 25-minute marathon you need to average 10:08 per mile.*

In the first ten weeks of training for this event, you should establish a base of 45 to 50 miles a week. A typical week's training during this period should include:

- one long stamina run of 12 to 15 miles at 10:45 to 11:30 per mile
- two endurance workouts on the track consisting of *one* of the following per workout:

  - 12 × 110 yards in 25 seconds, with a 330-yard recovery in between
  - 6 × 440 yards in 1 minute 50 seconds, with a 440-yard recovery in between
  - 3 × 880 yards in 4 minutes, with an 880-yard recovery in between
  - 2 × 1 mile in 8 minutes 30 seconds, with an 880-yard recovery in between

- four days of easy running (7 to 10 miles) at 10:45 to 11:30 per mile

Select one short-distance (110 to 440 yards) and one medium-distance (880 yards to 1 mile) endurance workout in each week's training.

During the first ten-week training period, you should attempt 3 or 4 races at distances of 8K to 20K. These races should replace an "easy running" day.

FINAL TEN-WEEK SCHEDULE

"Easy running" in this schedule is 10:45 to 11:30 per mile.

1st Week

Day

1 13 miles easy running
2 6 × 440 in 1:50 — 440 R
3 9 miles easy running
4 Rest day
5 10 miles in 95:00
6 3 miles easy running
7 6 miles incorporating 2 miles in 17:00

2nd Week

Day

1 14 miles easy running
2 6 × 220 in :50 — 440 R
3 5 miles easy running
4 3 × 880 in 4:10 — 880 R
5 4 miles easy running
6 Rest day
7 18 miles at 10:20 per mile

3rd Week

Day

1 4 miles easy running
2 10 × 110 in :24 — 220 R
3 6 miles easy running
4 8 miles easy running
5 Rest day
6 Rest day
7 Competitive effort: 10K to 20K

4th Week

Day

1 5–8 miles easy running
2 6 miles easy running
3 8 × 220 in :50 — 220 R
4 7 miles easy running

5 2 × 880 in 4:00 — 880 R
6 Rest day
7 20 miles easy running

5th Week

Day

1 4 miles incorporating 1 mile in 8:20
2 6 miles easy running
3 10 miles easy running
4 6 miles easy running
5 3 miles easy running
6 Rest day
7 Competitive effort: 10K to 20K

6th Week

Day

1 5 miles easy running
2 10 × 110 in :24 — 330 R
3 10 miles easy running
4 Rest day
5 10 miles in 97:30
6 Rest day
7 17 miles easy running

7th Week

Day

1 8 miles incorporating 3 miles in 25:30
2 5 miles easy running
3 4 × 440 in 1:48 — 440 R
4 5 miles incorporating 2 miles in 17:00
5 Rest day
6 Rest day
7 Competitive effort:10K to 20K

8th Week

Day

1 5 miles easy running
2 8 × 110 in :24 — 330 R
3 Rest day
4 10 miles in 97:30
5 3 miles easy running
6 Rest day
7 18 miles easy running

9th Week

Day

1 Rest day
2 12 miles incorporating 10 miles in 95:00
3 5 miles easy running
4 5 miles easy running
5 5 miles incorporating 2 × 1 mile in 8:20
6 4 miles easy running
7 10 miles easy running

10th Week

Day

1 5 miles easy running
2 5 × 220 in :49 — 440 R
3 4 miles easy running
4 4 miles easy running
5 Rest day
6 Rest day
7 4-hour 25-minute marathon

Choye Shannon, homemaker-grandmother. (Photograph by Bruce Glikin)

The 4-Hour 50-Minute Marathon

> *You are ready to train for a 4-hour 50-minute marathon if you can run:*
>
> > *1 mile in 8 minutes 45 seconds*
> > *10K in 61 minutes 30 seconds*
>
> *To run a 4-hour 50-minute marathon you need to average 11:04 per mile.*

In the first ten weeks of training for this event, you should establish a base of 35 to 45 miles a week. A typical week's training during this period should include:

- one long stamina run of 9 to 12 miles at 11:30 to 12:15 per mile
- two endurance workouts on the track consisting of *one* of the following per workout:

  - 10 × 110 yards in 26 seconds, with a 330-yard recovery in between
  - 5 × 440 yards in 2 minutes 5 seconds, with a 440-yard recovery in between
  - 2 × 880 yards in 4 minutes 20 seconds, with an 880-yard recovery in between
  - 1 × 1 mile in 9 minutes 15 seconds

- four days of easy running (4 to 6 miles) at 11:30 to 12:15 per mile

Select one short-distance (110 to 440 yards) and one medium-distance (880 yards to 1 mile) endurance workout in each week's training.

During the first ten-week training period, you should attempt 3 or 4 races at distances of 8K to 20K. These races should replace an "easy running" day.

FINAL TEN-WEEK SCHEDULE

"Easy running" in this schedule is 11:30 to 12:15 per mile.

1st Week

Day

1 12 miles easy running
2 5 × 440 in 2:00 — 440 R
3 6 miles easy running
4 Rest day
5 10 miles in 97:30
6 Rest day
7 6 miles incorporating 2 miles in 18:20

2nd Week

Day

1 12 miles easy running
2 6 × 220 in :55 — 440 R
3 3 miles easy running
4 2 × 880 in 4:20 — 880 R
5 Rest day
6 Rest day
7 17 miles at 11:15 per mile

3rd Week

Day

1 3 miles easy running
2 8 × 110 in :25 — 330 R
3 5 miles easy running
4 5 miles easy running
5 Rest day
6 Rest day
7 Competitive effort: 8K to 20K

4th Week

Day

1 4 miles easy running
2 6 miles easy running
3 6 × 220 in :55 — 440 R
4 5 miles easy running

5 2 × 880 in 4:20 — 880 R
6 Rest day
7 18 miles easy running

5th Week

Day

1 5 miles easy running
2 4 × 440 in 2:05 — 440 R
3 6 × 220 in :55 — 440 R
4 7 miles easy running
5 Rest day
6 Rest day
7 Competitive effort: 8K to 20K

6th Week

Day

1 3 miles easy running
2 8 × 110 in :25 — 330 R
3 6 miles easy running
4 10 miles in 97:30
5 3 miles easy running
6 Rest day
7 16 miles easy running

7th Week

Day

1 7 miles incorporating 2 miles in 18:30
2 5 miles easy running
3 4 × 440 in 1:55 — 440 R
4 3 miles easy running
5 Rest day
6 Rest day
7 Competitive effort: 8K to 15K

8th Week

Day

1 4 miles easy running
2 4 × 220 in :54 — 440 R

3   Rest day
4   6 miles in 66:00
5   3 miles easy running
6   Rest day
7   17 miles easy running

9th Week

Day

1   Rest day
2   10 miles in 97:30
3   5 miles easy running
4   5 miles easy running
5   4 miles with 2 × 1 mile in 9:10

6   4 miles easy running
7   10 miles easy running

10th Week

Day

1   4 miles easy running
2   5 × 220 in :53 — 440 R
3   4 miles easy running
4   3 miles easy running
5   Rest day
6   Rest day
7   4-hour 50-minute marathon

CHAPTER 9

Questions and Answers
for over-35 Runners

Q: Can running help lower my cholesterol level?

A: Yes. Besides that, being involved in an exercise program will un-
doubtedly increase your attention to many health-related topics
(such as diet), which will definitely affect your cholesterol.

Q: How old is too old to begin running marathons? Who are the oldest
marathoners? Their times?

A: There are 70- and 80-year-old marathoners. Derrick Turnbull ran
2:37 at age 60 in the South Australian Championships (averaging 6
minutes per mile!). The older divisions are beginning to be extremely competitive. As for beginning marathon training, it's not a
question of age but of health, desire, and commitment.

Q: Will running reduce my chances of developing osteoporosis after
menopause?

A: There is evidence that any weight-bearing activity will help fight
osteoporosis. Ask a doctor who knows something about running.

Q: I've heard that, as an older runner, I should race the longer distances because I have a better chance of doing well than in the
short distances. Is this true?

A: The aging process does affect more of the racing components used
in the shorter distances, especially speed and anaerobic endurance.
On the other hand, as we explained in chapter 1, this aspect of
aging can be compensated for and overcome to a significant extent.
And don't forget that "finding your distance" also involves your ratio
of slow-twitch to fast-twitch muscle fiber. So you may still run those

shorter distances well — especially compared to the other runners in your age group.

Q: What are the requirements for national masters competition?

A: You have to be 30 years of age or older to compete in The Athletics Congress (TAC) Masters track meets (runners 30–39 compete as "sub-masters"), and you have to be a registered member of TAC. TAC is divided into a number of regions, some of which have very active masters participation. As for time standards, you may be surprised to find that there are none, not even for national championships; if you're brave enough to enter, you can run, and it is certainly an experience worth having.

Q: I've always been able at least to *finish* my track workouts. But for about a month I haven't been able to, and now I don't want to think about them. What do you advise?

A: First assess your situation: are you under unusual stress, are you injured, are you overtrained, are you just plain tired, or are you actually ill? Once you've decided what the problem seems to be, try to estimate whether it will be over soon or if it's here for a while. If it looks as if it's likely to be a short-term problem, try to use the cushion built into the schedules (see the introduction to the schedules). If that doesn't work, and you remain "flat" (or if it looks like a long-term problem), raise your target time and go on to an easier schedule until you get the snap back in your legs. And if that doesn't work, see your doctor. You may be ill.

Q: I want to run just one marathon. Any advice?

A: Training for a marathon (while not the same as signing a contract for life) is a *serious* commitment, and not just something to do as a lark. Get checked by a doctor (preferably one who understands the mind-set of runners), allow yourself enough time, find a schedule that you're ready to run (see, for example, the 4:50 marathon schedule in this book), and start training.

Q: I am thinking about competing in a triathlon. How should I modify your schedules to complement my other training?

A: Do the tough cycling training on days when you *don't* have hard track work; however, I find that even tough swimming workouts can be combined with same-day track work, provided there's enough time between them. Also, you can't keep your mileage up as

Putting it all together: Andy Greenwood moves into masters competition. (Photograph by Bruce Glikin)

high as you could if you were only running; there's a trade-off. I usually lower the miles on my triathletes' recovery days and try to keep their track intensity relatively unchanged.

Q: I get extremely nervous at the starting line just before a race, and I think it affects the early part of my race. How can I stay calm until the gun goes off?

A: This is a common problem. Part of it is good — it's the excitement we look for when we think about racing. If it keeps you from competing well, however, you need to get it under control. Use the relaxation techniques we talk about in this book, and, as you continue to enter races, you'll find that your prerace jitters will go away.

Q: I'm 40. I'm in good health. I want to begin a running program. Do I really need to see a doctor?

A: Yes. Find one who is knowledgeable about running.

Q: Will an over-40 runner really run a sub-four-minute mile?

A: It's bound to happen. The question is who and when. If Wilson Waigwa can't get the last few seconds off his current 4:07, Rod Dixon, the great New Zealand runner, is rumored to have a 1-mile race already set up for him when he reaches 40 in July of 1990. If he doesn't make it, we bet on John Walker, who'll be 40 in 1991 — but who has also said that he would continue racing only through the next Commonwealth Games in 1990. As we mentioned in the introduction, there are a lot of very good masters runners now who can challenge four minutes. And — as the old racing expression goes — there's always one from the ranks.

Q: Are older runners more likely to get injured?

A: My experience is — perhaps surprisingly — that older runners get injured *less* than younger runners. Some of the older runners have been running for years and are obviously natural "survivors" — if they were easily injured they would have been out of the sport years ago. But even the older runners who are just beginning competitive training seem to have fewer injuries than their junior colleagues. Perhaps they're cagey enough to take it easy when they're under extra strain, or perhaps they are mature enough to realize that training is merely preparation for racing, and not a test of manhood.

But the bad news associated with age is this: If a masters runner *is* injured, you can be sure that he will heal more slowly, and be more prone to reinjury while recovering, than a younger runner.

Q: I'm over 30 and just beginning a running program. Can I ever be a really good runner, or am I already over the hill?

A: You might have missed something by not running during your "formative years," but there have been runners who took up running late in life and became great: Jack Foster started running in his late thirties and ran 2:11 for a marathon at 42; Priscilla Welch started running in her thirties and ran 2:26 in her forties. Other runners who started late may not have reached international stardom as Foster and Welch did, but they've been good enough to beat a lot of runners who had been training for much longer (as your authors can ruefully report). It's never too late to start. Good luck — and remember: Never, ever, pass your coach!

Index